MURDER ON THE HIGHWAY

Also by Beatrice Siegel

Lillian Wald of Henry Street

Sam Ellis's Island

George and Martha Washington at Home in New York

*The Year They Walked: Rosa Parks and the
Montgomery Bus Boycott*

MURDER ON THE HIGHWAY

THE VIOLA LIUZZO STORY

BEATRICE SIEGEL

FOREWORD BY ROSA PARKS

FOUR WINDS PRESS   NEW YORK

Maxwell Macmillan Canada *Toronto*
Maxwell Macmillan International *New York Oxford Singapore Sydney*

Four Winds Press
Macmillan Publishing Company
866 Third Avenue
New York, NY 10022
Maxwell Macmillan Canada, Inc.
1200 Eglinton Avenue East, Suite 200
Don Mills, Ontario M3C 3N1
Macmillan Publishing Company is part of
the Maxwell Communication Group of Companies.
FIRST EDITION
Printed and bound in the United States of America
10 9 8 7 6 5 4 3 2 1
The text of this book is set in Aster.
Book design by Christy Hale.

Library of Congress Cataloging-in-Publication Data
Siegel, Beatrice.
Murder on the highway : the Viola Liuzzo story / Beatrice Siegel. —1st ed.
p. cm.
Includes bibliographical references and index.
Summary: Presents the life of the civil rights worker
who was murdered shortly after the 1965 march from
Selma to Montgomery, Alabama, and discusses the rights of Afro-Americans
living in the South prior to and following her death.
ISBN 0-02-782632-5
1. Liuzzo, Viola, 1925–1965—Juvenile literature.
2. Selma–Montgomery Rights March, 1965—Juvenile literature.
3. Civil rights workers—Alabama—Biography—Juvenile literature.
4. Afro-Americans—Civil rights—Alabama—Juvenile literature.
5. Alabama—Race Relations—Juvenile literature.
6. Civil rights movements—Alabama—History—20th century—Juvenile literature.
[1. Liuzzo, Viola, 1925–1965. 2. Civil rights workers.
3. Selma–Montgomery Rights March, 1965. 4. Civil rights—History.
5. Afro-Americans—Civil rights.] I. Title.
E185.98.L58S57 1993
364.1'523'09761465—dc20   93-7148

*I would like to dedicate this book
to the grandchildren of Viola Liuzzo
—to Chris and Tony Dupree, and
to John and T. J. Herrington;
to Jacob, Violet, and James Liuzzo;
to Shadrick and Joshua Liuzzo;
to James Lauwers and
to Sarah and Christina Prado.
—B.S.*

CONTENTS

Viola Gregg Liuzzo *(The Montgomery Advertiser)*

FOREWORD

The story of Viola Liuzzo is very important to civil rights history. Her dedication and desire to join the 1965 Selma to Montgomery march must never be forgotten.

Thousands of men, women, and children participated in the march. They came to Selma, Alabama, not only from many areas of the United States, but also from other countries.

I joined the marchers in Montgomery. I had traveled by airplane with several members and officials of the UAW (United Automobile Workers) from Detroit, Michigan, to Atlanta, Georgia. From Atlanta we continued on to Montgomery by chartered bus, arrived early evening, and checked into a motel. Several of us ate dinner at the Harrises' restaurant—they were family friends of mine.

Sometime after dinner I took a cab to my friend Bertha Butler's home, with three other passengers who had also traveled from Detroit. I changed clothes at her home because my winter clothes were too warm, and she gave me a lightweight dress to wear on the march. We talked a lot, and I think I slept a little. She prepared breakfast for us at daybreak and asked someone to drive us to the City of St. Jude to join the marchers from Selma.

We called St. Jude a city, but it was a large Catholic church, school, and hospital built to service all people, regardless of race, creed, or color. St. Jude was four miles from the Alabama capitol and was the last rest stop for the marchers.

The large crowd gathered on the spacious grounds at St. Jude very much impressed me. It had been almost ten years since our struggle against racial segregation on the buses in Montgomery. Unfortunately, too many things had not changed in the minds of many white citizens. As we marched through the streets, hostile white people shouted insults and jeered at us. In some places there were foul odors (from stink bombs) in the air. There was no doubt in my mind that the struggle for racial peace and harmony had not ended. There was still much to be done to change the Cradle of the Confederacy to a city of freedom, racial harmony, and peace.

I walked the four miles to the capitol. As we approached the building we were jarred by the sight of the police and federal troopers. They were silent and looked threatening. The old visions of beatings, bombings, intimidations, and lack of protection returned. There was no welcome from Governor George Wallace or the mayor, but the thousands of people who kept marching around the capitol didn't seem to mind. The marchers stretched into the distance for as far as the eye could see.

At the capitol the march ended, and a program began, chaired by Reverend Ralph D. Abernathy. Dr. Martin Luther King, Jr., gave the keynote address. His message was most inspiring and eloquent.

I spoke also. Most of my brief remarks explained that the propaganda being circulated to the crowd and displayed on a billboard outside Montgomery about Dr. King being a Communist was untrue. The billboard showed a group of people at the Highlander Folk School pictured with the founder, Miles Horton, and indicated that the school supported communism. Highlander, in Monteagle, Tennessee, was in fact a school that was committed to racial harmony and world peace. Dr. King was never a student there as the antagonists indicated. He was the keynote speaker at its twenty-fifth anniversary program. I had been a student at Highlander, and my time there was the first time that I had experienced life without racial segregation and prejudice. I found it was very enjoyable to work and socialize in peace and harmony with people of all racial backgrounds.

Reading about Mrs. Liuzzo's early life, family history, and her sensitivity to injustice has given me a better understanding of her commitment to go to Selma and help with the march. She believed that action, not talk, was needed at that time. She volunteered to help prepare for the march in many ways, including working with the first-aid staff. Her desire to work as long as there was a need for her help unfortunately led to her tragic murder on the highway after the march.

The history of the racist and pro-slavery views of the white segregationists in Selma and their cruel, oppressive power against African Americans should be passed on, to both youth and adults. It is important to know how far we have come and also how far we still have to go.

We returned to the motel in Atlanta by bus and stayed for the night. My room was some distance from the UAW group. I was very tired and felt depressed. When I went to my room, undressed, and got into bed, it was impossible for me to fall asleep right away. I tossed and turned. When I did sleep, I dreamed of being shot at by a strange man in a field near some trees. When I awakened and turned on the television, I was shocked to see that Mrs. Liuzzo had been shot to death on the Selma to Montgomery highway. Her picture on the TV screen showed her to be young and attractive.

I believed Mrs. Liuzzo had not been told of the possible danger of her actions, although she had been advised by Reverend Abernathy, Reverend Hosea Williams, and others that the SCLC (Southern Christian Leadership Conference) could take care of transportation back to Selma. However, she wanted to help as long as she felt the need to do so.

This book proves that I was wrong in my belief. Mrs. Liuzzo had been warned by several people of the danger and cruelty of the KKK (Ku Klux Klan) and the hardened segregationists.

My earliest awareness of the KKK was shortly after the end of World War I when African-American servicemen returned home in the early 1920s. At the age of six, I sat on the floor at night by my grandfather's rocking chair. He kept his double-barrel shotgun nearby, in case the Klansmen invaded our home. We slept in our clothing due to our fear of the KKK night riders. He also kept the gun close by during the day. The Klan never did stop at our house, but we always feared they might. Neighbors in nearby communities suffered attacks.

The KKK dominated the Liuzzo murder trial. The defense lawyers for the three indicted Klansmen did everything in their power to discredit Mrs. Liuzzo's character. They accused her of being a Communist, a radical, and morally irresponsible. Anyone who fought for human rights was labeled a Communist—ironic, because the United States is supposed to be "one nation, under God . . . with liberty and justice for all."

Though the Klansmen were not convicted of murder, they were put in jail for ten years for violating Mrs. Liuzzo's civil rights. The verdict was a surprise to many people, especially civil rights workers. We were not accustomed to Klansmen being sentenced for anything, so a conviction was a step in the right direction.

In Detroit I went to the funeral home with some friends for viewing Mrs. Liuzzo in state. I also attended a memorial service for her and met her husband and children, extending words of sympathy to them.

This book tells a very intimate story. Viola Liuzzo's story shows that hatred makes all people victims of racism. Perhaps it will both encourage people to look within themselves and show us that we have lost too much talent because of racial prejudice.

Rosa Parks

CHAPTER ONE
THE QUEEN CITY

The settlers who moved into the Alabama Territory in the early nineteenth century were wealthy farmers looking for new soil in which to grow cotton. They found what they wanted in west central Alabama, where they lay claim to huge tracts of level land on a high bluff overlooking the Alabama River. The land was rich with black, fertile soil stretching east and west as far as the eye could see.

They called their town Selma, and from the earliest days made it a thriving center for the production of cotton and the slave trade. Each week during the season that stretched from September to April, hundreds of African men, women, and children were brought into Selma, lodged in huge wooden buildings especially erected for the slave trade, and auctioned off as field hands, carpenters, blacksmiths, and seamstresses. The

hard labor of slaves made it possible for plantation own-
ers to turn the lush, fertile soil into profitable cotton
fields. And the Alabama River running alongside the
town was a natural transportation belt for the shipment
of cotton south to Mobile and other ports. A network of
railways, industries, banks, and schools assured Selma
its place as a dominant southern city. To those bold,
ambitious settlers and their descendants, Selma became
the Queen City of the Black Belt.

During the Civil War, Selma maintained its influence
in a different way. It was developed into the main military depot for the Confederacy, producing ammunition
and artillery for those southern states determined to
hold on to slavery. The punishing defeat of the South in
the war left Selma destroyed.

Throughout the following decades, the city tried to
recapture its power by rebuilding its railways, banks,
industries, and cotton production. But there were only
minor successes. Selma never regained its prosperity
and influence—it was no longer the Queen City. And
one hundred years after the Civil War, it had settled into
a quiet rural southern town with its country club, movie
house, and shopping center. The white-columned mansions became only showplaces, reminders of the way
things once were.

The white elite, however, continued to dominate the
town's political and economic life just as it had in the
days of slavery. The African Americans, numbering
some 15,000, or about half the city's population, were
separated by race from the white community and neatly
roped off into segregated housing, schools, churches,
jobs, and social life.

One way the white elite held on to its power was to prevent African-American citizens from voting. If African Americans could not vote, they were power-less—powerless to change the political and economic structures. They could not vote against the local sheriff who beat them, or the whites who confined them to poor housing and streets piled high with uncollected garbage, or those who held them down with low-paying jobs and inferior education.

Though the Fifteenth Amendment, added to the U.S. Constitution after the Civil War, stated the right to vote could not be denied because of race, and though the Civil Rights Acts of 1957, 1960, and 1964 tried to pro-tect the right of African Americans to vote, still nothing had changed in the South. In 1961, in Dallas County, of which Selma is the seat, only 156 African Americans—or less than 1 percent of the voting age population—were registered to vote. But 9,000 white voters—or about 60 percent of voting age whites—were registered.

Why weren't more African Americans registered? It was an old story, one that never seemed to change, a story of how segregationists held on to their power. African Americans had to overcome a series of barriers that varied from town to town but had the same pur-pose: to keep them from casting a ballot. In Selma the registrar's office was usually open two days a month. On those days African Americans would line up to regis-ter, standing in line four or five hours only to find when they reached the office that it was closed for the day. Those who reached the registrar's desk were asked detailed biographical questions. If those answers were approved, they had to answer questions that tested their

7

knowledge of the U.S. Constitution and the fine points of local and state government. A typical question might be: What are the functions of the vice president and the Supreme Court? Most questions were so difficult that educated people could not answer correctly. Marie Foster, a dental hygienist, tried for eight years before she became a registered voter. Registrants, in addition, had to be accompanied by a registered voter as a character witness.

African Americans who were determined to vote were often threatened and intimidated. Frequently they lost their jobs. Sometimes they lost their homes when banks called in mortgages. Many who protested were beaten. Intimidation and violence were so successful that in some areas, such as nearby Lowndes County, no blacks were registered to vote though they made up the majority of the population.

On the surface it appeared as if African Americans accepted these conditions and perhaps at that time some of them did. As long as they stayed in their place, they were told, they were safe.

In the 1960s things began to stir. The civil rights movement was taking root in town after town. Freedom Rides, sit-ins, and massive protests rumbled through the South, weakening the foundations of the old social order and forcing history onto a new course.

Selma's quiet was shattered when African Americans made the town the center of their battle for the right to vote. The dramatic, intense struggle won newspaper headlines, filled television screens, and aroused the country. The struggle reached into the White House and into the U.S. Congress. That was when Selma made a new kind of history and joined Lexington, Concord, Harpers Ferry, Montgomery, Little Rock, and all other towns and cities across the country that became battle-grounds for freedom and justice.

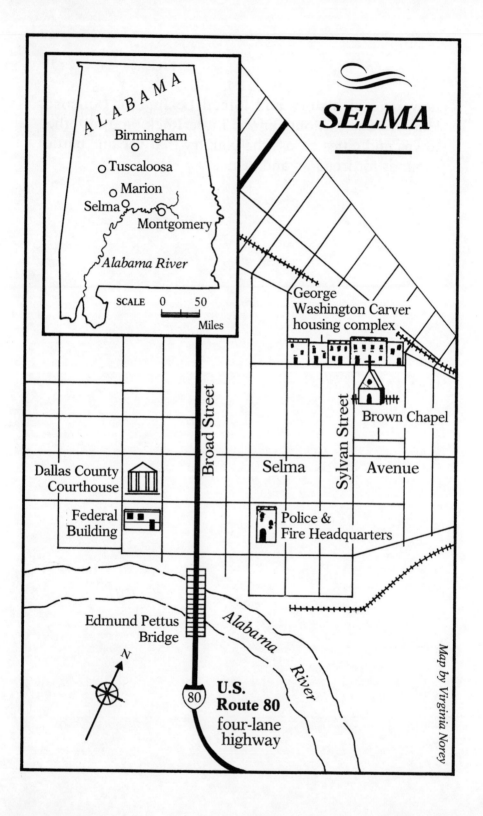

SELMA

ALABAMA

Birmingham

Tuscaloosa

Marion

Selma

Montgomery

Alabama River

SCALE 0 50

Miles

George
Washington Carver
housing complex

Brown Chapel

Broad Street

Sylvan Street

Selma Avenue

Dallas County
Courthouse

Federal
Building

Police &
Fire Headquarters

Edmund Pettus
Bridge

Alabama River

N

80 **U.S.
Route 80**
four-lane
highway

Map by Virginia Norey

CHAPTER TWO
THE STRUGGLE BEGINS

Two young people, the Reverend Bernard Lafayette and his wife, Colia Lafayette, arrived in Selma in February 1963 to start a Voter Education Project. Both twenty-two years old and Fisk University students, they were sent in by the Student Nonviolent Coordinating Committee (SNCC). The organization, made up of high school and college students from across the country, had participated in Freedom Rides, sit-ins, and other protests that were then changing the South.

In the slow, difficult process of educating people on how to win their right to vote, the Lafayettes had the help of a handful of seasoned African-American civil rights activists. Among them was F. D. Reese, a Baptist minister, teacher, and president of the Dallas County Voters League. Reese was outspoken in his demands for equality. Businesswoman Amelia Boynton opened her office to SNCC staffers. Mrs. Boynton and her husband were early leaders in the voter registration campaign. Lawyer J. L. Chestnut, Jr., also let SNCC people use his office. Mrs. Marie Foster started citizenship education classes to teach people how to fill out registration forms.

Mass meetings, marches, and protests brought the civil rights workers face-to-face with Dallas County Sheriff James G. Clark, Jr., known as a hard-line segregationist. For his tough defense of the social order, Clark was a popular figure in town. He had the backing of the White Citizens Council, made up of influential southerners dedicated to keeping blacks in their place.

Clark cut a striking figure walking around town in a helmet and short jacket, and usually wearing a pistol on each hip. Quick to use threats, violence, and arrests to keep blacks from making progress, he was a forbidding presence. To help him, he had a posse of men called deputies, armed and ready.

In the fall, organizer Worth Long replaced the Lafayettes, who went on to other projects. Overseeing Selma activity were two experienced SNCC leaders, James Forman and John Lewis. Though there were setbacks, Selma was slowly aroused from its long sleep. Through the daily hard work of SNCC staffers, young people—especially high school students—became impatient and restless. FREEDOM NOW! was their slogan, and they called for an immediate end to segregated toilets, lunch counters, water fountains, and schools. A sit-in at a Selma drugstore resulted in arrests and beatings. Fifteen-year-old Lulu Brown was shoved off a drugstore stool, and Willie Robinson needed seven stitches after being struck in the head. The incident sparked additional protests by Selma's high school and college students, who marched in the streets and filled meetings held in black churches.

SNCC felt strong enough to call its first Freedom Day on October 7, 1963, when 350 African Americans lined up in front of the Dallas County Courthouse in Selma to register to vote. On hand, only as observers, were agents of both the Federal Bureau of Investigation (FBI) and the Justice Department. Clark's deputies were reinforced by state troopers armed with guns, clubs, and electric cattle prods. A local photographer shooting pictures of everyone on the line assured that many would lose their jobs.

Through the heat of a sun-filled day, people stood in line from morning to late afternoon. For that day Sheriff Clark devised a new strategy, permitting no one to leave the line and return to it. It meant that no one could go for food or water or to use a toilet. Nor was anyone permitted to serve food and water to people on the line. Nevertheless two SNCC workers tried to do just that. They were quickly beaten and arrested.

Author James Baldwin witnessed the event and said at a meeting that the courage and determination of blacks that day "changed the course of the Freedom Movement in Alabama."

Newspapers began to take notice of the violence erupting in Selma. The beating of a CBS television photographer by Clark's deputies on Freedom Day put Selma in the spotlight. The following year, newly elected Mayor Joseph T. Smitherman tried to counteract the

African Americans lining up outside Dallas County Courthouse to register to vote *(Courtesy The Old Depot Museum, Selma, Alabama)*

negative publicity. He appointed a public safety director, someone with a "moderate" approach to race relations. The man appointed to the job was Wilson Baker, a former policeman and a teacher at the University of Alabama.

Though SNCC members had stirred things up in Selma, they nevertheless found white resistance unyielding after two years of intensive efforts. Mass meetings, arrests, beatings, and long lines on registration days did not significantly increase voting rolls. They agreed with other civil rights activists that new forces were needed to raise the movement to another level.

In January 1965 the Southern Christian Leadership Conference (SCLC), led by the Reverend Martin Luther King, Jr., sent staff into Selma to join SNCC in fighting for voting rights. The combined efforts of the two large civil rights groups brought unity to the African-American community by attracting new support from many church leaders and their congregations. The philosophy of the movement, nonviolent resistance, was the one Dr. King developed during the Montgomery bus boycott in 1955-1956.

On January 2, 700 African Americans gathered at Brown Chapel African Methodist Episcopal Church to hear Dr. King speak. The redbrick church with its twin steeples, located in the heart of the black community, had become the nerve center of the voter registration drive. That evening Dr. King told his audience that he had joined the battle for voting rights in Selma because of the stubborn white resistance and brutality. He supported SNCC in calling on the federal government to pass a voting rights bill as the only way African Americans would be able to participate in the democratic process.

Persuaded by Dr. King's eloquence, hundreds of blacks took to the streets to demand voting rights. Protests increased and so did police brutality. Over 1,000 civil rights protesters were arrested and jailed in Selma and nearby towns in early 1965.

In one incident Mrs. Amelia Boynton, who had succeeded in registering years before, was in the line at the courthouse to help a friend register. The highly respected Mrs. Boynton was a tall, stout woman, and she was a bit slow in moving along that day when a policeman grabbed her by the back of her collar and pushed her half a block into a patrol car. She was arrested and charged with criminal provocation. The incident received wide publicity as did the fact that Clark's deputies had arrested 67 marchers that day.

As the movement gathered momentum, it drew people from every profession and age group. Under the leadership of F. D. Reese, Selma's black teachers, known as a conservative group, staged a silent march to Selma's courthouse to demand voting rights. The group was cheered on by students.

College and high school students continued their persistent drive for equality. In one terrible episode, Sheriff Clark and his deputies tried to punish them by sending 165 teenagers on a two-and-a-half-mile forced march down a deserted country road. To make them maintain a fast pace, police hit them with clubs and jolted them with cattle prods. They were not permitted to rest for a single minute. Many students became ill, vomited, and wept with pain.

In other confrontations children as young as ten and twelve were caught up in the struggle and arrested. Louis Miller, a twelve-year-old and in the seventh grade, described for a *New York Times* reporter what it was like to be jolted with an electric prod. "It stung. We were getting on the bus after we were arrested. They said hurry. And used the cow prod." Why did he march? "For Freedom. To go where you want to go, do what you want to do, say what you want to say." Ten-year-old Reginald Mota, in the fifth grade, said, "Freedom means for your mother to get a better job, and for us to get better homes." Others said they wanted to be able to vote when they grew up.

The intense struggle spread to outlying districts, including the town of Marion, twenty-six miles from Selma. There, too, night and daytime marches filled the streets with a people's determination to win their rights.

On Thursday evening, February 18, a night demonstration at the Marion courthouse turned ugly when state troopers clubbed the marchers. Caught in the bloody confrontation was Jimmie Lee Jackson, a twenty-six-year-old laborer who had been trying to register to vote since he was twenty-one. He lived with his mother in a small house without running water. To escape from the troopers, Jimmie's mother and eighty-two-year-old grandfather fled into a café. Troopers followed, swinging clubs and smashing all the café lights. Jimmie saw police beating his mother and rushed to her defense. The trooper turned on Jackson and beat him to the ground while another trooper shot him in the stomach. Jimmie was rushed to the hospital, where he died eight days later.

An NBC television correspondent was also badly

beaten that day. The attack made headline news in the North. But the brutal slaying of young Jimmie Lee Jackson aroused the whole African-American community in Dallas County. Four thousand mourners walked in the rain to bury him in an all-black cemetery. At two funeral services, people demanded action. They were ready for a new kind of action—something that would make their voices heard.

CHAPTER THREE
BLOODY SUNDAY

Jimmie Lee Jackson's murder jolted the Selma civil rights struggle forward into a new dramatic strategy: Demonstrators would march to Montgomery, the state capital fifty miles away, to take their grievances directly to Governor George C. Wallace. Martin Luther King, Jr., would lead the march.

Governor Wallace not only refused to meet with a delegation of marchers, but he also banned the march as a danger to public safety. In the meantime letters, telegrams, and phone calls were reaching the White House in Washington, D.C., protesting police brutality and asking for a federal investigation into the situation in Selma. The federal government was being kept informed of conditions by agents of the Justice Department and the FBI, who were monitoring events. Dr. King himself met with President Johnson on

March 5 and was assured by the president that he would press for a voting rights bill.

Disregarding the ban on the march to Montgomery, SCLC leaders scheduled it for Sunday, March 7. SNCC did not officially endorse the action, but notified its members that they could participate if they so wished. Dr. King, it turned out, would not lead the march after all. There had been serious threats to his life and he was advised to stay away. He remained in Atlanta, Georgia, his hometown, attending to church business.

To provide protection for the march, SNCC staffers arrived with two-way radios and other equipment. They trained marchers in nonviolent resistance: how to let their bodies go limp in the event they were attacked and how to protect themselves from tear gas. Several doctors and nurses, flown in from New York City, gave brief courses in first aid and were on hand to provide medical care.

There was a great deal of debate in local government on how to deal with the march. Public Safety Commissioner Wilson Baker was worried about a "bloodbath." He was concerned that Sheriff Clark would stop the march by force and violence. Mayor Smitherman issued assurances that moderation would be used.

Though the march was legally banned, it did not stop some 600 African Americans and their white supporters from gathering together at Brown Chapel, the starting point, on the somewhat cloudy, cool morning of March 7. Marchers had with them backpacks, sleeping bags, small valises, and packages of clothes and food, whatever they thought they could carry on the fifty-mile walk.

They were led out of the church by two leaders, SNCC's John Lewis and SCLC's Hosea Williams. In columns of two, marching alongside one another and singing freedom songs, they walked through the black community and into downtown Selma toward the Edmund Pettus Bridge, three-quarters of a mile away. Following the marchers were four ambulances. Just before the marchers reached the bridge, they passed about thirty of Clark's deputies. The ambulances were stopped and not permitted on the bridge.

The Edmund Pettus Bridge arches high over the Alabama River. It slopes upward toward the halfway mark and down to the other side, where it connects with U.S. Route 80 and the road east to Montgomery.

Not until the marchers walked onto the bridge and reached its crest did they see what awaited them on the far side. Blocking the highway and standing shoulder to shoulder forming a solid wall were fifty Alabama state troopers in uniforms and helmets, carrying clubs, whips, and gas masks. In back of the troopers were more of Sheriff Clark's posse, some of them on horseback. On the sidelines were about fifty whites verbally hassling the marchers, while in the distance about fifty blacks quietly watched. In a car nearby sat Clark and Colonel Al Lingo, state director of public safety, known as a man of action.

Just as the marchers walked over the crest of the bridge, down on the other side, they heard the order "STOP!" It was shouted by Major John Cloud, head of the troopers. The marchers came to a halt and heard Major Cloud say through a bullhorn, "This is an unlawful assembly. Your march is not conducive to public safety. You are ordered to disperse and go back to your church or to your home."

Hosea Williams asked if he could talk to the major. "There is no word to be had," said Cloud. "You have two minutes to turn around and go back to your churches," he said.

One minute later, when no one moved, Major Cloud called out, "Troopers, advance!" At the order a phalanx of troopers slammed into the marchers, beating them with clubs and whips. Whites on the sidelines cheered the troopers on. The first marcher to fall was John Lewis, who was clubbed over the head and suffered a fractured skull. Mrs. Amelia Boynton and her friend Mrs. Marie Foster were beaten and fell to the ground. Others tried to escape by rushing back over the bridge. They dropped what they carried, scattering their belongings along the way. Troopers followed, horseback deputies trampling the crowds of fleeing, screaming, wounded marchers. In another assault troopers sent a dense gray cloud of tear gas over the crowd. No one had the chance to practice what had been taught. Marchers fled, pursued by Clark's mounted posse who followed them into the grounds of the George Washington Carver housing complex near Brown Chapel.

On the march was eight-year-old Sheyann Webb. As fast as her young legs would carry her, she fled back across the Pettus Bridge through the streets to her home in the housing complex. "They had beaten us like we were slaves!" was the way she described it in a memoir written years later, *Selma, Lord, Selma*. Troopers were carrying rifles "like soldiers in a war zone," she wrote. They beat people all the way into the housing project, stomping over the grounds, making it a danger zone instead of a zone of safety. "Get all of them," Jim Clark shouted to his deputies. Ambulance crews, trying to help the wounded, were stopped by the police. Reporters, too, were kept away but photographers using telephoto lenses captured the bloody event on film.

Clark's men prevented Brown Chapel from being used as a sanctuary. Only after the intervention of Public Safety Commissioner Wilson Baker were Clark's deputies forced from the church grounds.

Those who reached the church sat weeping and dazed, staring straight ahead, trying to deal with the savage beating and their fears and rage. Next door in the parsonage, turned into a first aid station, doctors and nurses were patching up the wounded, soothing burning eyes, cleaning cuts and bruises. Serious cases of fractured legs, arms, and ribs, head gashes, and mouth wounds were treated at Good Samaritan Hospital. The admissions book at the hospital showed that John Lewis was admitted at 4 P.M. with a fractured skull. Seventeen people were hospitalized that day.

While the wounded were being treated and others were trying to regain their strength and courage, the phones were busy. The first calls went to Martin Luther King, Jr., to notify him of the ambush and beatings. Newspaper reporters began to spread the news across the country about the march in Selma on March 7. The day would become known as Bloody Sunday.

Bloody Sunday—a woman beaten unconscious by state troopers is helped by friends *(UPI/Bettmann)*

CHAPTER FOUR

THE TURNAROUND

On the evening of March 7, ABC television interrupted the viewing of its regular Sunday night movie to announce a special news bulletin. Flashed on the screen were photos of Selma police and troopers attacking the quiet columns of marchers on the Edmund Pettus Bridge, and horses stampeding into the dazed crowd.

Those who did not get the news on television read about Bloody Sunday the next day in newspaper headlines. The *New York Times* said, ALABAMA POLICE USE GAS AND CLUBS TO ROUT NEGROES. The *Washington Post* reported, TROOPERS ROUT SELMA MARCHERS. Newspapers in small and large cities wrote about the assault while photographs relayed the emotional message of innocent people being violently attacked. By Monday the whole country had seen or read about the brutality of the Selma police.

Selma itself was the scene of round-the-clock meetings attended by Dr. King, James Forman, John Lewis,
Ralph Abernathy, and countless aides. They decided to
call another march to Montgomery for Tuesday,
March 9. Dr. King, trying to rouse the conscience of the
nation, sent telegrams to clergy of all faiths asking them
to join him in Selma. "No American is without responsibility," he wired, and though the people of Selma would
continue their struggle, it was only "fitting that all
Americans help bear the burden." Calling another
march was a way of notifying the country that the
African-American people would not step back.

In response to Dr. King's call and the nationwide publicity, priests, nuns, ministers, and rabbis rushed to
Selma. So did hundreds of students, workers, and professionals. They dropped classes, jobs, and housework,
and found their way to the small rural town by car, bus,
train, and plane. The hundreds who joined the crusade
were housed in nearby homes, churches, and wherever
space was available.

While the country was being informed of Bloody
Sunday and supporters were pouring into the small
town, the subject was being discussed at the highest
level of the national government. The country could not
face another bloody encounter. Telegrams and phone
calls besieged the nation's capital urging the government to intervene and protect defenseless people.
Members of Congress also voiced their concern.

Though supporters were pouring into Selma, the decision to march was undergoing serious debate. Judge
Frank Johnson of Montgomery had legally barred the
march and urged its postponement until hearings could

be held. He warned that another march might again be met with bloody violence. The federal government sent down two mediators to work out a solution. But neither LeRoy Collins, director of the Federal Community Relations Service, nor John Doar of the Justice Department could persuade black leaders to postpone the march. Nor did they have any success in urging Sheriff Clark to act with restraint. The White House and others tried to work out a compromise between the civil rights leadership and Governor Wallace, who remained opposed to the march. It seemed hopeless. The African Americans would not be terrorized into silence. On the contrary, they were determined to move forward. Adding to the tensions were the death threats received by Dr. King.

Through the night of Monday, March 8, into the early dawn of Tuesday, March 9, African-American leaders met and talked to thrash out the decision: to march or not to march. As the sun rose on the city of Selma, the choice was made: They would march to Montgomery that very day.

Everyone was on edge, filled with both fear and determination. Many were bolstered by the dramatic show of support of hundreds who continued to show up at Brown Chapel. In the nation, too, tensions were high. Millions were riveted to television sets on the day of the march. They watched 2,000 marchers line up outside the church. Leading the column were Dr. King, James Forman, and James Farmer of CORE (Congress of Racial Equality). In the front lines were actors, clergy, public officials, and wives of congressmen. Singing freedom songs, banners and flags carried by the stal-

27

wart, they marched through the business section of town to the entrance to the Edmund Pettus Bridge. There a U.S. marshal stopped them and read aloud the order from Judge Johnson requesting that they postpone the march. Dr. King refused, and led the marchers onto the bridge up to its crest, and then down to the far side. There stood Major Cloud once again at the head of a phalanx of armed troopers blocking U.S. Route 80. Cloud stopped the marchers and said they could go no farther. Dr. King asked whether they could pray and sing. Cloud agreed. For a few minutes, 2,000 marchers knelt or stood in prayer and sang "We Shall Overcome." In a surprise move, King then turned around and led the marchers back across the bridge, up the city streets, and back to Brown Chapel.

What was that all about? Why did Dr. King turn back, or make a turnaround, as the day's action would come to be called?

Neither the marchers, nor the public, nor some of the leaders knew of the intense pressure exerted on Dr. King to force him to postpone the march to Montgomery until the federal government could guarantee security. During hasty phone talks between the White House and Dr. King, between the White House and Governor Wallace, and between a judge in Montgomery and the government, a compromise was worked out to enable both sides to claim victory. The compromise called for the marchers to walk to the Edmund Pettus Bridge. At the point where they saw armed state troopers massed at the far side of the bridge, they would turn back. On the condition that marchers would not confront the troopers or push their

The turnaround—troopers stop marchers at the far side of the Edmund Pettus
Bridge *(UPI/Bettmann)*

ıto the highway and the road to Montgomery, the troʌ ers agreed not to use force.

Though Dr. King's decision created dissension among African-American leaders and organizations as well as among the ranks of the marchers, the compromise seemed to hold for the moment.

But Bloody Sunday was still uppermost in the minds of many, especially in Washington, where forty-three members of the House and seven senators spoke in defense of the Selma protestors. A picket line outside the White House swelled to 600 demanding protection for southern activists and urging the passage of a voting rights bill. Members of SNCC staged sit-ins at the Justice Department. And finally President Johnson himself spoke on the matter, promising legislation that would assure the right of every citizen to vote.

Among those who had responded to Dr. King's call to the clergy was the Reverend James J. Reeb, a Unitarian minister from Boston, who worked on inner city projects. He marched along with other clergy in the Tuesday walk to the Edmund Pettus Bridge. Somewhat confused by the turnaround, he was planning to return to Boston. But his colleagues in the Unitarian Universalist faith urged him to stay on with them.

The evening after the march, the Reverend Reeb had dinner with two other ministers at Walker's Café, a black eating place frequented by civil rights workers. At about 7:30 P.M., the three left the café. In the dark street, unsure about how to return to Brown Chapel, they lost their way and wandered into an unfamiliar neighborhood. The Reverend Reeb was on the curbside and his two colleagues alongside him when four white men accosted them and called out, "Hey, niggers, hey, you niggers!" Realizing they were in trouble, the ministers quickened their pace but not before one of the assailants swung a club or lead pipe and smashed it over Reeb's head. Reeb's colleagues were attacked with bare fists and fell to the ground. The three men were helpless on the pavement and their attackers continued to beat them, shouting, "Here's how it feels to be a nigger down here." Though it was early evening, no one was on the street. Finally Reeb's friends, the Reverends Orloff Miller and Clark Olsen, were able to get to their feet and help Reeb to his.

Reeb was in terrible pain and complained that his head hurt as the three stumbled back to civil rights headquarters. One look at Reeb convinced the staff that Reeb was seriously hurt. They rushed Reeb into a makeshift ambulance and drove him to a small segregated hospital. A doctor, seeing how critically injured Reeb was, arranged for his immediate transfer to the better-equipped Birmingham University Hospital. There doctors diagnosed a massive skull fracture. Two days later, on Thursday, March 11, the Reverend Reeb died. Four men were arrested for the attack.

The country exploded in anger at Reeb's death. White Americans were beginning to understand the hatred and violence confronting African Americans, especially those who lifted their voices. Less than three weeks earlier Jimmie Lee Jackson had been attacked. His death had not received the nationwide attention accorded the murder of the Reverend James Reeb, but the continuing assaults, violence, and hatred tapped into the conscience of millions of Americans and a wave of protests swept the nation. In Selma protesters held a round-the-clock prayer vigil. On college campuses demonstrations, marches, and meetings shook the quiet halls of learning. In Boston, Reeb's hometown, as well as in New York, San Francisco, and Detroit, there were mass demonstrations. Protesters around the country—workers, professionals, men, women, students—all called on the federal government to arrest the criminals, protect the civil rights activists, and pass a voting rights bill.

CHAPTER FIVE
VIOLA LIUZZO

On Sunday evening, March 7, Viola Liuzzo and her husband, Jim, were in their home in Detroit, Michigan, watching television news at 11 P.M. Like millions of others, they saw unfolding on the screen the events that had taken place in Selma, Alabama, on Bloody Sunday. As they watched police and state troopers beating defenseless people on the Edmund Pettus Bridge, tears ran down Mrs. Liuzzo's face. She raged in anger and sadness at the needless violence.

Viola Liuzzo was beginning to put her life together now that the dust storm that had blown her off course most of her life had settled. She could sit back, think, and plan for the future. Age thirty-nine and the mother of five children, she had recently returned to school as a part-time student at Wayne State University. Having dropped out of school in the tenth grade, she had hard work before her. The excitement of college studies made her dream—perhaps someday she would become a physician. For the present it was rewarding to be taking classes in literature, creative writing, and other subjects that interested her. But the images of the brutal events she had seen on television troubled her so much that she was distracted from her studies.

Viola Liuzzo thought of herself as a child of the South and suddenly it was as if she was called home.

She was born in the dusty, small coal mining town of California, Pennsylvania, on April 11, 1925. Her parents, Heber Ernest Gregg and Eva Wilson Gregg, named their first child Viola Fauver. Her father, a World War I veteran and a school dropout in the eighth grade, worked as a coal miner. The job ended when his right hand was blown off to the wrist in a mining accident. Though her mother held a teaching certificate from the University of Pittsburgh, she could not always find a job in her profession.

A few years after Viola's birth, the whole country was plunged into the Great Depression of the 1930s. Massive unemployment, hunger, and homelessness forced thousands to travel back roads looking for work. The Gregg family was part of the pilgrimage. They journeyed through the South, settling for a time in Georgia, and then went on to Tennessee, where Mr. Gregg's parents lived. In Tennessee Mrs. Gregg was able to get a teaching job.

Though Viola's childhood was one of hardship, a

hand-to-mouth existence in one-room shacks without running water, she preferred to remember the fun she had. A favorite sport was climbing up and down the trunks of trees. It was a special treat when she could buy a can of chicken noodle soup with pennies she saved from odd jobs. During those years in the South, a sister, Rose Mary, was born in 1936.

In the poor neighborhoods where Viola Gregg lived, schools were not well equipped and teachers were too burdened to pay special attention to needy youngsters. Vi, as she was called, would remember that the family moved around so much, she never started and finished a school term in the same city. She learned her basic ABCs, and despite the urgings of her parents, both of whom cherished the need for education, she dropped out of school in the tenth grade. She was then attending St. Mary's Junior High School in Chattanooga, Tennessee.

Though Mr. Gregg had been a school dropout, he nevertheless had educated himself and was a very well read man. Perhaps he hoped Viola would not repeat his mistakes. Though good-natured and generous, he had little patience with his daughter. Viola, with her gray-blue eyes and honey-colored hair, was beautiful, energetic, and filled with enthusiasm for harmless pleasures. But her father did not approve of her love for dancing or her late evenings out. When she could no longer tolerate the friction in the family, Vi rebelled by running off to marry a man more than twice her age. After one day the marriage was annulled. That was in 1941, the year the country was lifted out of the economic depression by the onset of World War II. To find work, many people

35

Viola Gregg in an elementary-school photo in Atlanta, Georgia (third row, second from right) *(Courtesy Penny Herrington)*

moved north toward the factories manufacturing cars, bombs, and ammunition for the Allied cause.

The Gregg family—including Viola—also moved north and settled in Michigan, where Mrs. Gregg became the essential breadwinner. Factory work paid much better than teaching, and she found jobs at first in a bomb factory, and later at the Ford Motor Company in Ypsilanti. Home for a while was a housing project of barrack-style buildings. Later the Greggs moved into a row house in Willow Run, where Ford had a factory.

Viola, now on her own, picked up odd jobs as a waitress until she married again in February 1943. She was eighteen and her husband, George Argyris, was again twice her age. He operated a cafeteria for a business firm. In June 1946 Viola gave birth to a daughter, Penellipi (called Penny), and in 1948 to Evangeline (renamed Mary Eva). When the marriage ended in divorce in 1950, Viola gained custody of the two children.

Custody of the children was one thing. Raising them as a single working woman was another. To ease the burden, the two little girls were sent to live with Viola's parents in Willow Run. Both Penny and Mary had fond memories of their grandparents who, they said, inspired them to be good students.

For Viola this was a difficult time: her children in one city, she in another, working at a job that did not tax her mind but did provide a living.

She was working as a waitress at the New Olympia Bar and Restaurant in Detroit when she met Anthony James Liuzzo. Jim, as she called him, was a persistent admirer, a man thirteen years older than she, and a business agent for Local 247 of the International Brotherhood of Teamsters. He was tall, heavily built, and genial. She was small, lively, cheerful, and attractive. When her relationship with Jim became serious, she converted to his faith, Catholicism.

Toward the end of 1950, Vi and Jim were married. Soon after, the family was united when Penny and Mary came to live with their mother and stepfather. Vi and Jim added two sons to the family, Thomas in 1951 and Anthony, Jr., in 1955. In 1956 Jim legally adopted Vi's two daughters and the family was legally one. To it was added another child, Sally, born in 1958.

Mrs. Liuzzo spent weeks in the hospital while she was pregnant with Sally, a last child she so desperately wanted. An overactive metabolism, which interfered with her pregnancy, had already caused three miscarriages. To help her hold on to the baby she was given strong medication.

Sally, at birth, was so frail and limp, the doctors said she probably would not live. If she did, they said, she would not be normal; she would never be able to lift her head. Shocked by the news, the Liuzzos had a priest administer the last rites. But it was not in Mrs. Liuzzo's nature to accept such a verdict. She was determined to save her new little daughter.

She lavished her full attention on the infant, carefully feeding and nurturing her. When the child was eight months old, Mrs. Liuzzo proudly showed a neighbor how Sally could hold up her head. At three years of age, Sally was pronounced normal. Doctors called it a miracle. Apparently the strong medication administered to Mrs. Liuzzo for her metabolic problem had interfered

Viola and Jim Liuzzo with three-year-old Sally *(The Detroit News)*

with the nourishment of the fetus. The newborn infant, severely malnourished, appeared permanently damaged. But Mrs. Liuzzo's determination gained for Sally a normal life.

The family lived in a small house on Marlowe Street in Detroit when Sally was born. She was four when they moved into a more spacious home on the same street. The redbrick house with white trim and a fieldstone front was on a tree-lined street, and the Liuzzos became part of the middle class interracial neighborhood.

Mrs. Liuzzo's energy was boundless at times. "She radiated life," was the way a friend put it. Everybody who met her felt her warmth. Neighbors found her generous and good-natured. She was always doing something, collecting for a charity or helping others. "There wasn't a thing she wouldn't do for anybody," said a neighbor.

She loved not only people but animals. To the annoyance of her husband, who did not share her love for pets, she would bring home stray dogs and cats. Often birds lived in the house, among them a mynah bird and a parakeet. For a period she collected antiques, filling the house with a mix of odd dishes and a vintage gramophone. Nor was she ever too tired to bundle up the children and take them on walks in the woods where she told them about the marvels of the natural world. "Adventure discoveries," she called them. In the summer of 1964, Viola took Tony and Tommy on a camping trip to Tennessee. She tried to explain to her two sons, as they sat at an open fire surrounded by trees and stars, that the rich natural surroundings were their true heritage, not the crowded, busy city streets. Always

The Liuzzo family home on Marlowe Street in 1965 *(The Detroit News)*

an enthusiast, she filled the house with rock samples when she became interested in geology.

Sometimes the children found their mother deep in history or philosophy books. She would read to them from the works of Henry David Thoreau, trying to teach them why she found this American philosopher and nature writer so important. She would try to explain what Thoreau meant by "civil disobedience," a way of protesting government actions he considered unjust. And all day the children would hear the classical music their mother loved. At night came different sounds, the jazz their father preferred.

Holidays inspired Mrs. Liuzzo to extraordinary heights of enthusiasm. One Halloween, for example, she dressed up in a costume, used cosmetics to paint a grotesque face, and stole around the outside of the house peering through windows, scaring the children. And on one particular Saint Patrick's Day, she served a green dinner, dying the potatoes green.

"She filled each moment of her life," was the way Mrs. Sarah Evans remembered her. Mrs. Evans was Mrs. Liuzzo's close friend and family housekeeper. They met in Detroit when Viola was nineteen and Mrs. Evans worked in a grocery store. She educated Viola to the indignities she suffered because she was an African American and made Viola sensitive to the continuing insults stemming from racism. Through Mrs. Evans, Viola Liuzzo became a member of the National Association for the Advancement of Colored People (NAACP), a large membership organization dealing with the problems of racism.

The care of her large family filled Mrs. Liuzzo's life

and was often exhausting. Knowing how much his wife loved the countryside, Mr. Liuzzo surprised her with the purchase of a simple, rustic cabin. But weekends with the family did not bring much relaxation.

There were days when her enormous energy drained away, leaving her as limp as a flower tossed by the wind. At such times the children were accustomed to their mother curling up in bed for a few days, needing quiet and sleep to restore her energy. And there were darker periods, too, when only a fragile boundary separated everyday life from a strange unreality. Getting in the car and driving away was often an escape for Viola Liuzzo, a healing process. On one occasion, she drove off without notifying the family. After two days Jim Liuzzo reported her to the police as missing. She was located in Montreal, Canada, at the home of old family friends. In notes to Jim at the time, she appeared to be acutely depressed and not quite coherent. But those incidents, frightening as they were, faded into the general tenor of her days.

Essentially she had boundless enthusiasm for what life had to offer. She thought nothing of driving to New York City and did so at one time with Sarah Evans as her companion. They visited the Statue of Liberty and attended a seminar at the United Nations in the spring of 1964.

But despite a full life, something was missing. Viola Liuzzo was beginning to redefine herself, looking for her own voice. The tenth-grade school dropout regretted her lack of formal education, and in 1961 she enrolled as an evening student at a career training school called the Carnegie Institute of Detroit. There she studied to become a medical laboratory assistant and medical secretary.

In applying her energy and intelligence to her classwork, she developed into a high achiever. The school director would recall that she tape-recorded lectures so that she could go over them at home. Somewhat older than other students, she became a caring figure, opening her home to those who needed a place to study. At examination time she invited students to her house for all-night study sessions. Julia Deaton, a Carnegie Institute student, remembered those night sessions. "If it wasn't for her, some of us wouldn't have gotten through school," she told journalist Anthony Ripley for an article in the *Detroit News*.

Viola Liuzzo blossomed at the Institute and in March 1962 she graduated as one of two top honor students, with a grade average in the upper nineties. At graduation she was awarded a gold trophy. Sitting in the audience swelling the applause were her proud husband and children.

CHAPTER SIX
"WE SHALL OVERCOME"

Graduating with top honors from Carnegie made it easy for Mrs. Liuzzo to get a job. In June of 1962 she started work at the Parkview Medical Center. At home running the household and caring for the children was her housekeeper and good friend Mrs. Sarah Evans.

During her year at Parkview, she found labor practices there unfair. At one point she turned over her salary to a secretary who she thought had been unjustly fired. Then she went on a one-woman campaign to expose working conditions at the facility. As was her style, she moved decisively. One evening she remained in the building after others had left, and called the police. She notified them that she planned to steal a microscope. She gave the police the license number of her car and the direction in which she would be traveling. When the police caught up with her, they found no microscope. Nevertheless, Mrs. Liuzzo insisted on being taken to the police station. Because her husband was a known labor leader, she got media attention, which she used to publicize conditions at Parkview.

Viola Liuzzo felt justified in what she did. A moral commitment to justice was part of her personal philosophy. It did not matter that others might disagree with the methods she used to call attention to injustices. Ingrained in her was a compelling force, a moral monitor that forced her to speak up when an unfair act was committed.

Mrs. Liuzzo had no trouble finding another job and soon she was employed part-time at Sinai Hospital, where she worked in the tissue laboratory. Her superior was a visiting research scientist from Nigeria.

The two years of schooling at Carnegie and her experiences in medical laboratories sharpened her appetite for more education. She was thirty-seven years old in 1962, living a comfortable life in suburban Detroit, a busy woman—a wife and the mother of five children. But she wanted a larger vista, more options for her future. In her vision was the possibility of college.

Wayne State University was not far from where she lived. The urban campus with its mix of buildings, from gothic to modern, was familiar to her. It was a school for continuing education that drew working people to part-time study programs. She applied for admission to Wayne State in May 1962. Though a high school dropout, she did so well in the placement exam that she was accepted as a "conditional" student with credentials valid for one term. Could she make it? Could she apply herself to classes in biology, French, geology, and English composition? The record shows that she dropped a couple of difficult courses but did well enough in the others to be readmitted for another semester. By January 1964 she won unconditional admission and was allowed to take a full program of courses.

Because of her own experiences as a school dropout, Viola Liuzzo embarked on a campaign that challenged the school system. She was convinced that children should be required to remain in school until age eighteen, not until age sixteen, which was then the law. She discussed her point of view with the Detroit Board of Education. They agreed with her but made it clear they could do nothing about it at the time.

She undertook her own campaign to change the board's regulation. To dramatize the situation, she withdrew her two sons, Thomas and Anthony, then twelve and nine years old, from school and tutored them at home. She also took Mary, an A student, out of high school. When the children had been absent for forty days, the school board cited Mrs. Liuzzo for breaking the law. In the early morning of June 16, 1964, she was arrested in her home on Marlowe Street for "failure to send the children to school." When the case came to court, the Board of Education asked that the case be dismissed. But Mrs. Liuzzo insisted on pleading guilty. She was fined fifty dollars for court costs and put on one year's probation. Her arrest, her only one, appeared on the police record.

The year 1964 had been tumultuous for Mrs. Liuzzo. A reordering of priorities put on top of the list the need to fight for equality for all people. She ended a poem she wrote in December 1964 with these words:

> Truth is not Christian, Jewish, Hindu or
>   Buddhist.
> What is true for one man is true for all men.
>   Just as
> there is no such thing as Christian medicine,
>   Jewish biology or Hindu.

In the spring of 1965, Viola Liuzzo was taking courses in Shakespeare and philosophy at Wayne State. She was moving along a newly defined track and the future lay open before her. What was she thinking as she walked from one campus building to another? Was she able to define herself in a new way, as an independent, educated woman?

The spring season lagged behind that year, wet, wintry winds rattling leafless trees and whipping along the open spaces of the college squares. The new spring was slow and uncertain but new voices were loud and clear. The war in Vietnam was being hotly debated as was the continuing round of struggles in the South, where African Americans were demanding the right to vote. Not only was the college campus filled with unaccustomed political activity, but the city itself was in movement. Detroit was the home of the United Automobile Workers of America (UAW), a trade union that was a powerful force. Equally important was the large African-American population that lived and worked in the city.

By the spring of 1965 Wayne State was boldly proclaiming its support of the southern civil rights movement. Several young people had gone down south under the leadership of the Student Nonviolent Coordinating Committee and had returned to report on their experiences.

Though a long-time civil rights supporter, Mrs. Liuzzo had not participated in any meetings or protests. She was, however, increasingly preoccupied with the brutality inflicted on black citizens trying to gain equal rights. When bombs struck the Sixteenth Street Baptist Church in Birmingham, Alabama, in 1963, killing four young children, she and Sarah Evans comforted each other during those difficult days. It upset Mrs. Liuzzo that so much violence was loose in the country, that defenseless people were the victims of the uncontrolled hatred of white segregationists. Members of the Ku Klux Klan, brought to trials for bombs and murder, escaped the hand of the law only to continue their outrageous acts.

She was troubled enough to look for answers. One source of comfort was the church. Though a Catholic, she began attending meetings at the liberal First Unitarian Universalist Church of Detroit, housed at the edge of the Wayne State University campus. The church was noted for its social activism. Some of its members had been south and inspired the church membership to organize civil rights protests.

The church had a broad range of programs. On one occasion Mrs. Liuzzo dropped daughter Penny off at a meeting for the college-age group. Though Viola Liuzzo did not become a member of the church, she found it comforting to listen and participate in the liberal talk.

The Reverend Nancy Doughty, who knew Mrs. Liuzzo

slightly at the time, thought she was perhaps looking for something in tune with her own development—looking for a way to expand as an independent person.

On other occasions Mrs. Liuzzo turned to the Episcopal chaplain at the university. The Reverend Malcolm Boyd had participated in southern civil rights struggles and was actively involved in Detroit in support groups then developing. He held weekly meetings in his home where students discussed political and social issues and where he counseled troubled youngsters.

Through newspapers and television, Viola Liuzzo kept herself informed and she began to share conversations on campus with sympathetic students who were equally upset by the unfolding events in southern towns. A new camaraderie was springing up, a bonding among those who talked about doing something, about going south or holding campus meetings or protesting in some way the violence against African Americans.

After Bloody Sunday on March 7, Detroit held one of the largest demonstrations in the country. Ten thousand people, led by Governor George Romney and Mayor Jerome Cavanaugh, marched through the streets of Detroit demanding federal government protection for civil rights workers. When the Reverend James Reeb was murdered in Selma, thousands of people again took to the streets, urging immediate federal action.

Voices from all parts of the country demanded that Congress pass a voting rights bill. It was not enough that President Johnson sent a spray of flowers to the Reeb family with a condolence message. The country demanded more.

At Wayne State as well there was a new surge of

protest actions. Students who had been to Selma spoke at meetings. Over 500 teachers and students signed petitions demanding federal intervention. Hundreds went to Washington to join the march and the continuous vigil in front of the White House. On the campus itself, 250 students staged a sympathy protest march. Part of the group marched into town to the federal building, where a delegation met with the Federal Bureau of Investigation. Participating in the demonstration and march was Viola Liuzzo, her first such action. She marched along with the others, singing the civil rights song "We Shall Overcome." That step on March 12 changed Viola Liuzzo from a passive supporter to an active participant in the civil rights movement.

CHAPTER SEVEN
FROM SELMA TO MONTGOMERY

Meanwhile, in Selma, Alabama, plans were being made for a third march to Montgomery. A delegation hoped to meet with Governor Wallace to urge equal voting rights for black people. The date set for the event was Sunday, March 21. The march would be an enormous undertaking involving thousands of participants. Working on detailed plans were committees discussing shelter, food, security, and medical care. By careful estimates the march would take four nights and five days. Though plans were going forward, uncertainty still hung over the project because both city and state governments had banned the march. The hearing on a permit was then before Federal Judge Frank M. Johnson in Montgomery, and a decision was expected any day.

The increased civil rights activism around the country and especially at Wayne State deeply affected Viola Liuzzo. She had a nagging sense that she had to do more than she was doing. Her classes in Shakespeare and philosophy did not seem urgent. What was urgent was the need to do her share in the national emergency. It meant going down to Selma. Nothing in her past made such a move familiar. Except for the recent Wayne State march, she had never participated in group political or social activities, finding it more comfortable to do things her own way. But she was ready to become part of a mass movement.

The president of the United States also found the situation urgent. On Monday evening, March 15, at 9 P.M., Lyndon Baines Johnson addressed both houses of Congress and the nation. Seventy million listened to the televised talk. In a ringing speech, he called for support of the voting rights bill then before Congress. Referring to the protests and violence in Selma and throughout the South, he blamed the events on the inability of African Americans to vote. "It is wrong—deadly wrong to deny any of your fellow Americans the right to vote in this country," he said. Referring to the "outraged conscience of a nation," he urged the speedy passage of voting rights legislation. The president announced his support of the demonstrations in Selma, commenting on the courage of black Americans to risk their lives and safety in the fight for freedom. These actions, he said, have won the support of the nation. At the end of his speech, he invoked the powerful words of the freedom song, announcing in his Texas drawl, "We shall overcome."

That Monday evening Viola Liuzzo attended a meeting at the home of the Reverend Malcolm Boyd. He called these get-togethers "meet and talk and share" discussions. As usual his apartment was filled with some forty to fifty people, many of whom sat on the floor. The talk was intense, often impassioned. Young people told of their experiences in the civil rights struggle and how they felt about the mounting atrocities in the South. For many the struggle had become the center of their lives. They were prepared for sacrifice. They knew the risks involved in going south to live and work with African Americans.

Viola Liuzzo sat there gripped by the recital of personal experiences confirming her own need to join the movement. She was not a great presence, the Reverend Boyd would recall. "The ordinariness of her," he would say, was what made an impression. She was one of the group, "very sincere, an idealist, like the others. One could say," said the minister, that she was "a truly religious person, not explicitly religious, but religious in a profound sense. She had a deep spirituality, almost a saintly quality. She was ready to take risks for what she believed in." According to the Reverend Boyd, Viola Liuzzo was seeking the truth, looking for spiritual truth, "the manifestation of God in a broad rather than in a narrow way."

The next morning, Tuesday, Viola Liuzzo quietly put a few clothes into a shopping bag. Only to Sarah Evans did she confide that she was going to leave for Selma. "Everyone was going," she said, and she would be driving down with other students.

Mrs. Evans pleaded with her not to go. It was risky, she said. But Mrs. Liuzzo was determined. She discussed the care of the children with Mrs. Evans and said she would be back in a few days.

When she left for school that afternoon, Mrs. Liuzzo stashed the shopping bag in the family car, a 1963 blue Oldsmobile sedan, and drove off. Early in the evening she phoned home to speak to her husband, Jim. She was leaving for Selma, she told him. He was shocked and upset. It seemed to him a dangerous undertaking and he begged her to come home to discuss it. That was exactly what Viola Liuzzo wanted to avoid. She knew that Jim would not approve and she knew how persuasive he could be. "It's everybody's fight," she told her husband. "There are too many people who just stand around talking," she said.

Daughter Penny picked up the extension and heard the telephone conversation. She knew how determined and hardheaded her mother could be and her crisp voice on the phone indicated that nothing would change her mind. But Penny, like Jim and Mrs. Evans, was worried. She had a terrible premonition. She broke into the telephone conversation and pleaded with her mother not to go. "Mom," she said, "I have a terrible feeling I'm not going to see you anymore. Let's trade places. Let me go instead of you."

"I need to be there and I don't want to talk about it anymore," replied her mother. She told Penny, then eighteen years old, to take care of her brothers and sisters. Mary, the second oldest, had married and moved to Georgia, and Mrs. Liuzzo commented that she hoped to visit Mary before she returned home. "I want to see how Mary is doing," she said.

For Viola Liuzzo uncertainty had disappeared and everything had come together. The need to go to Selma was so compelling that she no longer had a choice.

Though she expected to travel south with others, apparently that plan did not materialize, and she drove her Oldsmobile down to Selma herself, leaving Wayne State University campus on Tuesday, March 16.

Word was broadcast over radio and television the next day, Wednesday, that the long-awaited decision by Judge Johnson was handed down. He approved the march from Selma to Montgomery with a few restrictions. On the four-lane sections of the highway, the number of marchers was unlimited. Where, however, the road narrowed into two lanes, as it did on a long stretch between the two cities, the number of marchers was limited to 300.

Brown Chapel had become the vital center for the march. Receptionists, staff, medical personnel, and the leadership crowded into the church's facilities to correlate the many facets of activity surrounding the huge undertaking. The parsonage next door was also put to use as were the nearby business office and home of Mrs. Amelia Boynton.

Viola Liuzzo was among the thousands who reached Brown Chapel the week of the march. She registered and was given housing with Mrs. Willie Lee Jackson in the nearby George Washington Carver apartments. Hundreds of families opened their homes to civil rights supporters during that week.

At the church Mrs. Liuzzo was assigned to the reception desk, where she greeted newcomers. Several remembered her as being solicitous in caring for them. The Reverend Jack Mendelsohn wrote in his book, *The Martyrs*, that Mrs. Liuzzo was extremely well liked both at the Jackson home and at the reception desk. He quoted the Reverend Carl R. Sayers, rector of St. Stephen's Episcopal Church in Birmingham, Michigan, who said, "When we arrived we were tired and frightened. . . . Mrs. Liuzzo saw that . . . and went out of her way to be nice to us. I was amazed to see her doing so many things . . . always to help people. She was a doer."

Mrs. Boynton also thought highly of Mrs. Liuzzo. She recalled that Mrs. Liuzzo came to her house during a staff meeting and that she was "an attractive young woman, outgoing with a personality anyone could approach."

"She was a very sweet one, no stranger," was the way Mrs. Jackson put it, talking about Viola Liuzzo, who became part of her family for a few days in Selma. Mrs. Jackson was impressed with the way Mrs. Liuzzo "picked up" the family's routine. She was especially helpful in the care of the children and knew what to do about the newborn grandson who was then five weeks old. Mrs. Jackson would always remember the evening the infant was crying without stop, and she was ready to take the child to the doctor. But Mrs. Liuzzo had a different idea. The child, until then fed only by bottle, was hungry, she said. And she went downstairs to the nearest grocer to buy jars of baby food. When she returned, she fed the infant additional food, and sure enough the baby stopped crying.

Mrs. Jackson would also recall that each evening Mrs. Liuzzo went across the street to a neighbor's house to make a phone call to talk to her husband and children.

She had not arrived at the Jackson home weighed down with luggage. All she had with her, said Mrs.

Jackson, was a shopping bag filled with clothes. She came to Selma because she thought she could help. "She was not only sweet, she was courageous," said Mrs. Jackson.

At Brown Chapel, Mrs. Liuzzo met Leroy Moton, a nineteen-year-old civil rights activist who coordinated the work of the transportation committee. The six-foot-three-inch, very thin young man was a familiar figure to the SCLC staff. Moton lived in the Carver apartments, held a job in town as a barber, and spent all his free time at Brown Chapel. At some point in their talks, Viola Liuzzo agreed to make her car available to the committee. It would be used to transport civil rights workers from one place to another. It would also be used to carry marchers who could not walk the full distance. After the march the car would be of service in transporting marchers from Montgomery back to Selma.

CHAPTER EIGHT
"A SHINING MOMENT"

Over 3,000 people gathered in Selma on Sunday, March 21, to participate in the march to Montgomery. Many northern whites, eager to be helpful, shared the common tasks required to make the undertaking succeed. They worked on toilet and water facilities, shelter, security, food, finances, and as medical personnel.

The national publicity and the support of President Johnson assured maximum security. When Governor Wallace refused to provide protection, claiming it would be too costly, the president had 1,900 members of the Alabama National Guard placed under federal supervision. He also had military police, FBI agents, and U.S. marshals flown into Selma. Troops were on the alert at army bases in Georgia and North Carolina.

The night before the march, army jeeps rolled

through the town carrying soldiers armed with rifles and bayonets. Two field hospitals were staffed and ready for use on Sunday morning. Army helicopters stationed at the nearby airstrip were available. Every crossroad on the highway was guarded, every part of the road searched for troublemakers. Military personnel were poised and ready to ride up and down the highway throughout the days of the march. Security would come to an end only when the march itself was completed, when the marchers reached Montgomery and dispersed.

According to one marcher, security was so tight and solid, she felt as if she were surrounded by a fortress wall.

The huge press coverage captured for the public the drama and spirit of the event. Simeon Booker in *Ebony*

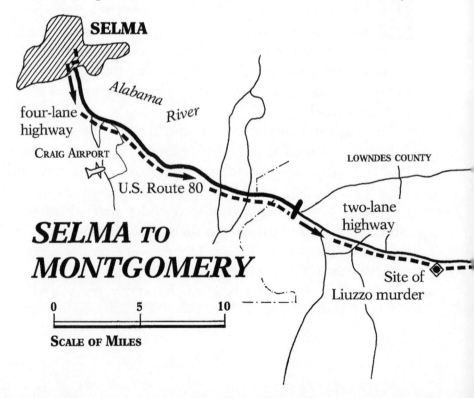

SELMA

Alabama River

four-lane highway

CRAIG AIRPORT

LOWNDES COUNTY

U.S. Route 80

two-lane highway

SELMA TO MONTGOMERY

Site of Liuzzo murder

0   5   10

SCALE OF MILES

magazine called it "a people's army . . . dynamic and electric . . . a landmark in group might." Writer Jimmy Breslin called it "the march of little people . . . little people who stood up in the sun and asked for a thing which was theirs and never had been given to them because they are black."

This people's army was made up of blacks and whites from every class, profession, and religion: doctors, nurses, workers, priests, nuns, rabbis, housewives, and students from over fifty colleges. They had come to Selma because they felt passionately committed to the fight of African Americans for their freedom and equal rights. They said the violence against African Americans and their supporters—the murders, beatings, and brutality—had to stop. They came to bear witness, and to do the grinding chores needed for the march. And they

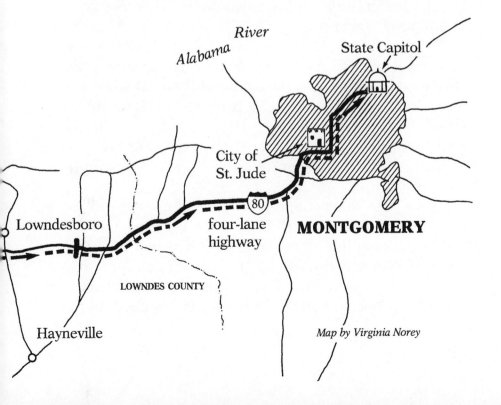

Map by Virginia Norey

were there to put their bodies on the line, for they knew that people of goodwill had to accept risks.

Viola Liuzzo was part of the historic moment. She, too, came because she knew it was not enough to talk, that she had to act in support of her beliefs.

On the sun-filled Sunday, Viola Liuzzo was among the 3,000 as the march got under way, unfolding like a colorful ribbon. Rippling in the soft breeze were U.S. flags, banners, and placards. In the lead was a line of African-American marshals with linked arms. They kept the crush of reporters away from the notables. Among those walking with Dr. King were the United Nations diplomat and Nobel Peace Prize winner Ralph Bunche, U.S. District Judge Constance Baker Motley, John Lewis of SNCC, Coretta Scott King, and SCLC leaders Andrew Young and the Reverends Ralph Abernathy and James Bevel. Also in the front lines was Jimmie Lee Jackson's grandfather, Cager Lee.

The march started down Sylvan Street, turned onto Selma Avenue and then onto Broad Street, through the business area, and onto the Edmund Pettus Bridge. The marchers walked across the bridge onto U.S. Route 80—the road to Montgomery—walking together "to the promised land." Lining the streets were hundreds of African Americans celebrating the show of black unity and power.

On the first afternoon, marchers covered seven miles, walking steadily along the four-lane highway with its yellow dividing line. By evening they reached the property of David and Rosa Belle Hall, an African-American couple who, despite their fears, allowed the marchers to use their property. Four huge tents were pitched on the fields while food, prepared in the kitchens of African-American churches by volunteer women and men, was ferried over. First aid trucks brought medical personnel to clean and soothe blistered feet and to provide other medical care.

At 8 A.M. on Monday morning, after a hasty breakfast of oatmeal and coffee, the marchers stepped forward on their second day. Spirits were high though many complained of bruised and swollen feet and poor sleep on hard ground. Their steady pace was interrupted when the march reached the two-lane segment of highway, where their number was reduced to 300 for several miles in accordance with legal restrictions. In the core group led by Dr. King, Coretta Scott King, and SCLC and SNCC staffers, including James Forman and John Lewis, were twenty whites. They included a nun from Kansas City, wearing her habit, and a mother and son from a poor rural section of Georgia. The son was deaf and blind and had to be helped along. There was also a minister from a small Massachusetts town and Jim Letherer, a settlement-house worker from Saginaw, Michigan. Supported on crutches, he hobbled along, a cheerful, robust man. "I believe in brotherhood," he said. "My handicap is not that I have only one leg. It is that I cannot do more to help these people vote." Actor Gary Merrill was also on the line of march, walking alongside a fifty-six-year-old farmer from a neighboring county.

The 300 marchers moved through the forbidding landscape of Lowndes County. Those who knew the reputation of the area were fearful of snipers even though security was tight. The overcast sky made the day seem

Among the dignitaries in the front line of the march to Montgomery (starting second from left): A. Philip Randolph, John Lewis, Ralph Abernathy, an unidentified man, Ralph Bunche, Martin Luther King, Jr., and Coretta Scott King *(Laurence Henry Photographer's Portfolio/Schomburg Center for Research in Black Culture/ The New York Public Library/Astor, Lenox, Tilden Foundations)*

A mother and son from rural Georgia among marchers on the two-lane segment of highway through Lowndes County *(Laurence Henry Photographer's Portfolio/ Schomburg Center for Research in Black Culture/The New York Public Library/ Astor, Lenox, Tilden Foundations)*

more ominous as they walked past swampland and a jungle of trees draped with drooping graybeard moss, trees that looked mournful even on a sunny day.

Lowndes County, a relic of the old South, boasted of its deeply entrenched segregationist policies. Fewer than eighty-six white families owned 90 percent of the land, and whites controlled all political offices. The rich lived in old, stately mansions in a county known as one of the poorest in the whole country. In this hidden and dangerous racist world, not a single African American could register to vote even though African Americans made up 80 percent of the population. They were prevented from registering by the threats and intimidation of the Ku Klux Klan, who dominated the countryside, especially the county seat of Hayneville. The KKK had undertaken to defend and protect the way of life of southern white America, guaranteeing the control of the county to the small white aristocracy.

While marchers held their banners high and their lively freedom songs rippled over the countryside, across fields, and through the woods, two helicopters flew low, searching for snipers. Always in sight of the marchers were army personnel, the FBI in unmarked cars, and army jeeps racing up and down the highway.

On the second day, marchers covered some seventeen miles of curved and hilly roadway until they reached the property of Mrs. Rose Steele, a store owner. When first approached the seventy-year-old widow had hesitated about permitting the marchers to camp on her fields. But she thought about it and figured she did not have much to lose, and a great deal to gain. "I almost feel like I might live long enough to vote myself," she commented.

Military police guarding the roadway on the second day of the march *(AP/Wide World Photos)*

Mile after mile the marchers walked on the road to Montgomery, covering eleven miles on the third day under a cold, steady rain. A few held umbrellas, others used plastic head covers, while many walked along in sodden clothes. That night, on the Gardner farm, tents were pitched on muddy fields. Everyone was exhausted and bogged down in muddy shoes and wet clothes. Again medical personnel took care of bruised feet and bodies, trying to ease the exhaustion. And again food was transported from Selma.

Though the weather on the fourth day was a mixture of sun and rain, spirits revived. Thousands had arrived by bus and car to join the marchers, who were once more on a four-lane highway.

Covering some sixteen miles, a tide of people entered the final night's resting site at the City of St. Jude, a huge complex run by a Catholic order on the outskirts of Montgomery. The redbrick buildings housed a church, a school, and hospital. Huge flat fields surrounded the buildings and became home for the final night of the march.

Viola Liuzzo had joined the march the first full day and returned to Selma for the night. She lodged with the Jackson family each night and during the day spent an hour or two at Brown Chapel. Evenings she phoned home to talk with the family. Because her car was being used by SCLC staff, early Wednesday morning Mrs. Liuzzo took a bus from Brown Chapel and joined the march at St. Jude's, becoming one of the thousands who had taken over the fields. Cars were parked wherever possible and a crowd had begun to assemble in the late afternoon before a platform set up with lights and

The church at the City of St. Jude *(Courtesy Paul Robertson)*

loudspeakers for a gala festival of entertainment. On hand were Harry Belafonte, organizer of the festival; Sammy Davis, Jr.; Joan Baez; Peter, Paul, and Mary; actor Anthony Perkins; comedian Dick Gregory; conductor Leonard Bernstein; and many more. The entertainment went on until 1 A.M. Photographers and journalists sent their coverage to the far ends of the world.

In the basement of the church, which had been turned into a first aid station, Mrs. Liuzzo was working with the medical staff. Father Cassidy of Chicago noticed her and how helpful she was. She declined a cot offered her for the night, saying a marcher should have it. She would sleep in her car, she said, which was then at St. Jude's.

That Wednesday night Mrs. Liuzzo phoned home and asked her husband to wire fifty dollars. She planned to visit her daughter Mary in Georgia before returning home. "Everything is all right," she said. "I'm very happy. Don't worry." Her husband urged her to be careful. He cautioned that the end of the march did not always mean that the danger was over.

The next morning, Thursday, Mrs. Liuzzo asked Father Tim Deasy, a priest at St. Jude's, whether she could observe the march from a high floor of the church so that she could get a full view of the size and spirit of the crowd. He took her up to the church tower and from its narrow windows she could see thousands falling into line and moving onto the highway for the final four-mile walk to the state capitol.

Returning from the tower, Mrs. Liuzzo was assailed by an attack of anxiety. She had a sense of doom; a terrible premonition overwhelmed her. Something awful was going to happen, she told Father Deasy. Speaking in a low, anxious voice, she said someone would try to kill Governor Wallace and then put the blame for the murder on the marchers. She communicated her fears to another priest and some nuns. A moment later she excused herself and said she was going into the church to pray. When she emerged, she seemed calmer and she joined the line of marchers to Montgomery.

Spread out across the widths of the streets, the marchers walked through the black ghettos of Montgomery into the downtown business area. They turned the corner at Court Square, with its historic fountain, and walked up Dexter Avenue, past the Dexter Avenue Baptist Church where Dr. King had his first ministry. The streets were filled with the sounds of music, "The Battle Hymn of the Republic" and "God Bless America." Colorful placards and banners carried messages: UAW [United Automobile Workers] SUPPORTS FREEDOM, read one poster. Others showed places of origin: Hawaii, Europe, Canada. Marchers could see flags waving above the state capitol: the state flag of Alabama and the stars and bars of the Confederate flag. Only among marchers did the U.S. flag predominate.

While marchers awaited the speakers, singers Harry Belafonte and Joan Baez were at the microphone urging the crowd to join them in the song "You've Got to Move When the Spirits Say Move."

Twenty-five thousand excited, joyous people filled the plaza in front of the state building. But the capitol building itself was barred by a line of police and troopers standing shoulder to shoulder at the bottom of the white marble stairs. The delegation that had hoped to meet with Governor Wallace was told they had to wait until the rally was over and the marchers dispersed.

Chairing the rally was the Reverend Ralph Abernathy, who introduced a list of prominent dignitaries as well as representatives of the major civil rights groups and unions—among them A. Philip Randolph of the Brotherhood of Sleeping Car Porters, Walter Reuther of the UAW, Ralph Bunche, Roy Wilkins, head of the NAACP, and Whitney Young of the Urban League. Cheering the crowd with her brief talk was Rosa Parks, who had joined the marchers for the final four miles and whose courageous act ten years before had launched the historic Montgomery bus boycott.

Finally the Reverend Abernathy, in his florid oratory, welcomed Dr. King, whom, he said, God had sent to "the heart of Egypt, to tell the pharaoh, 'Let my people go.'"

Dr. King, eloquent and impassioned, sounded the theme of the struggle: the suffering of his people. He praised the marchers. "Some of our faces are burned from the sun; some of us have slept in mud; we have been drenched in the rain . . . our bodies are tired, our feet are sore," he started by saying. "They said we would not get here, but we are here, and we are not going to let anybody turn us around."

Dr. King touched everyone with his somber recital of the history of the black struggle. He commented that the Civil Rights Act of 1964 gave blacks some dignity but no strength because it did not give them the right to vote. He called Selma, Alabama, a "shining moment in American history," when the pilgrimage of blacks and their white supporters joined hands. The fight against segregation in Alabama was costly, he said, but "we are on the move now . . . we are moving to the land of freedom." He called for an end to segregated housing and segregated education and for an end to poverty. "The battle is in our hands," he said, but he foresaw difficulties, "a season of suffering . . . there are jail cells waiting for us." He urged his listeners to commit themselves to nonviolence and work for friendship with white people. "How long will it take? Not long," he said, "because truth pressed to earth will rise again." He repeated to a crescendo of wild applause, "How long will it take? Not long, because mine eyes have seen the glory of the coming of the Lord. . . . His truth is marching on."

"SHE HAD NO FEAR..."

iola Liuzzo had marched from St. Jude's to the plaza in Montgomery. For part of the way, she had removed her shoes and walked barefoot as many others did. She was disheveled-looking from sleeping in her car and having no adequate facilities for a cleanup. But everyone else who had walked miles on hot paved roads under a sunny sky was disheveled. It did not matter. A current of solidarity bound marchers to one another. This was what it was all about, the excitement of being among thousands fighting for a just cause. She listened to Dr. King, strengthened by his eloquence. The fifty-four-mile walk from Selma to Montgomery, and the rally and unity of tens of thousands of African Americans and their white supporters had to be a highlight of the civil rights movement.

Her companion on part of the walk was Leroy Moton, the young civil rights worker she had met in Selma. He had used her car for errands, and once again they discussed the need to ferry marchers back to Selma. Mrs. Liuzzo was determined to stay on after the march so that she could continue to help.

By late Thursday afternoon, the great walk was over and thousands made their way to buses, trains, planes, and cars to travel home. Security, too, began to disperse. After the march Viola Liuzzo went over to the Dexter Avenue Baptist Church, where SCLC staff was arranging for marchers to return home. They had buses ready to transport them back to Selma.

J. T. Johnson of the SCLC staff remembered Viola Liuzzo. "She had no fear . . . and would do anything," was the way he recalled her.

Both Mr. Johnson and the Reverend Hosea Williams tried to convince Mrs. Liuzzo that they were able to deal with transporting marchers back to Selma and did not need her help. Others, too, tried to convince her that adequate arrangements had been made. But she was adamant. "She did what she wanted to do. She wanted to be helpful up to the last minute," Mr. Johnson recalled.

Notwithstanding the advice, Mrs. Liuzzo picked up her car at St. Jude's that late afternoon and with Moton sitting beside her, she drove four passengers—three women and a man—in her Oldsmobile along Route 80. At the local airport, she dropped off the male passenger and continued toward Selma.

Her car with the Michigan license plates had already been noticed on the highway when she had stopped at a white-owned gas station for gas. She thought nothing of curious incidents. A car in the rear flashed its lights on high and left them that way, shining into the Liuzzo car. "Two can play at this game," Mrs. Liuzzo said. She deliberately slowed down until the car behind her picked up speed and passed her. Farther along Route 80, a car pulled up alongside the Liuzzo car while the one in front slowed down. "Boxing them in," was the way one of the passengers recalled the incident.

After she dropped the remaining passengers at the George Washington Carver apartments, she and Moton separated for dinner. They met again in the early evening to return to Montgomery. It was exactly 7:34 P.M. Moton had noticed the time on a bank clock when Liuzzo stopped her car at a traffic light on the way out of town and a car with four white men drove up alongside her. The car's occupants observed the white woman sitting alongside a black man. In segregated Alabama it was a risky thing to do, a danger signal. Segregation meant a separation of the races. African Americans could not sit at the same lunch counter as whites, drink from the same water fountain, or use the same toilets. They surely could not sit alongside whites in an automobile. Race mixing, as it was called, often led to explosions of racial hatred and violence.

But Viola Liuzzo was not aware that she was being careless. Even if she knew that sitting next to a black man in an automobile was dangerous, would she have obeyed the restriction? She hated everything that made a mockery of human relations.

The four white men who observed her, however, were members of the Ku Klux Klan. "Let's get them!" one of the men said, and the driver proceeded to follow the Liuzzo car.

When she hit the highway, U.S. Route 80, Mrs. Liuzzo became aware that her car was being followed. To lose the pursuing car, she put her foot on the gas and increased her speed to eighty and then to ninety miles an hour. The road was desolate that evening, with few cars and no security, no army trucks or federal troops. Things looked grim when she came to Lowndes County and she could not shake the tail. The countryside was eerie in the dark, with its moss-laden trees and swampy ditches. She was speeding along, humming the freedom song "We shall overcome—someday," when she reached a lonely spot called Big Swamp Creek. In the darkness of the night, the other car closed the distance and pulled up alongside the Oldsmobile. While Viola Liuzzo was humming a freedom song, a young man poked a gun outside the rear window. In that instant Viola Liuzzo turned and looked at him, humming, staring. The man pulled the trigger. Shots rang out. Bullets crashed through the window and pierced her skull. Viola Liuzzo died instantly while a fusillade of bullets shot holes in the car.

She fell against the wheel, spurting blood over Moton. When he heard the glass shatter, he grabbed the steering wheel and slammed his foot on the brake. The car swerved off the road, hit a ditch, and came to rest against a barbed wire fence. Moton turned off the lights and ignition and tried to get Mrs. Liuzzo to speak. Just as he realized that she was dead, he noticed the car returning and pulling up alongside. Aware of the danger, he quickly fell to the floor, pretending to be dead, while the occupants of the other car shone a searchlight into the front of the Liuzzo car and then sped off.

Viola Liuzzo's car with bullet-shattered window on the driver's side *(AP/Wide World Photos)*

Desperate and terrified, Mr. Moton at first tried to get the attention of passing cars by honking his horn. When that failed, he ran down the road toward Montgomery. He ran almost three miles before he saw a truck that he recognized as belonging to the civil rights movement. He hailed it and climbed in, shouted a few sentences about a woman being murdered, and passed out. He was driven to Brown Chapel, where he told about the shooting. Civil rights workers took him to police head-quarters to report the murder.

CHAPTER TEN

"SHE GREW SO HIGH..."

At ten minutes after midnight, the phone rang in the Liuzzo home in Detroit. The family was asleep. Jim Liuzzo answered the phone and heard a voice say, "I have some very bad news for you. Your wife has been shot."

"Is it serious?" Mr. Liuzzo asked.

"It's critical," the voice answered. After a pause, "She's dead."

The ringing of the phone awakened the children. They heard their father screaming, "My God, Mom's been shot. Someone killed Mom."

All reason fled. Sanity vanished into the night and over the Liuzzo household descended a nightmare world that never completely went away. Television crews and reporters enveloped the house, friends and neighbors poured in, calls were made to Viola's parents and daughter in Georgia, Tony saw his father crying for the first time, and Mr. Liuzzo's sister came to the house and took the two youngest children, six-year-old Sally and ten-year-old Tony, home with her. Sally wanted to know, "Why couldn't Mommy have just died from being old?"

Sometime during that painful night, Mr. Liuzzo tried to get through to President Johnson at the White House.

But the news had already reached the president and at 12:40 P.M. the next day, he appeared on live nationwide television to announce the murder and the arrest of four suspects, all members of the Ku Klux Klan.

The president spoke for the nation, once again shaken by the senseless murder of a civil rights worker. "Mrs. Liuzzo went to Alabama to serve the struggle for justice," he said. "She was murdered by the enemies of justice, who for decades have used the rope and the gun and the tar and feathers to terrorize their neighbors." In an angry voice, the president declared war on the Klan, informing the nation that he planned to send an anti-Klan bill to Congress calling for an investigation into the KKK's "hooded society of bigots." The president went on to explain that these bigots strike at night because their hateful deeds cannot stand the light of day. He issued a warning to members of the Klan that they had better get out of the Klan organization because, he said, "Justice must be done," and he meant to see that it was.

The shot that killed Mrs. Liuzzo touched raw nerves. She was the first white woman to be killed in the civil rights struggle. The collective conscience of the people in the United States was already stricken about conditions of African Americans asking for the simple right to vote, already smarting over the brutality and violence in the South. Since 1963 Alabama's racial violence had resulted in eleven murders; Mrs. Liuzzo's was the third in the voter registration drive. Telegrams and phone calls again flooded the White House and congressional offices, demanding federal intervention and protection for civil rights workers.

The president used the Liuzzo murder to hasten Congress's passage of the voting rights bill then before it. He had already spoken personally to Mr. Liuzzo on the phone to express his and Mrs. Johnson's sympathies. Visiting the Liuzzo home on behalf of the national government was Vice President Hubert Humphrey. Michigan's Governor George Romney came to express the state's sorrow and to announce that Monday, March 29, and Tuesday, March 30, would be official days of mourning. Romney said, after the visit, that Mrs. Liuzzo "gave her life for what she believed in, and what she believed in is the cause of humanity everywhere."

While dignitaries, friends, neighbors, and relatives filled the house, the members of the Liuzzo family walked around barely able to contain their grief. Mrs. Evans came to stay with the children, helping as best she could, but she herself suffered over the loss of her good friend. Viola's parents, the Greggs, who drove up from Fort Ogelthorpe, Georgia, tried to understand the strange sequence of events—a daughter who went down south to participate in a struggle for black voting rights and whose body was now being shipped from Selma to a funeral home in Detroit.

Flowers, money, and phone calls poured in from all over the country and sacks of mail were dropped off at the Liuzzo home and at the Teamsters Union headquarters. Not all calls and letters expressed sympathy. There were calls filled with hatred. Even in the neighborhood, reactions were mixed. Many praised Viola Liuzzo's generosity and bravery; others wanted to know how she could have left her children to go down south on such a risky mission. She was no good, a few said. Some could not understand why a white woman would endanger her life trying to help black people.

The criticism was so severe that the Reverend Malcolm Boyd, the former Wayne State University chaplain, came to Mrs. Liuzzo's defense. He had known her as a student and remarked that it was people like Mrs. Viola Liuzzo who made up the moral backbone of the civil rights movement, that they were so committed to freedom that "they were really prepared to die for it."

Members of the family's parish church were also critical. When it was announced that a solemn requiem mass would be held for the slain woman, callers wanted to know, "How could the church grant a Christian burial to a divorced woman?"

The diocesan weekly newspaper, the *Michigan Catholic*, concluded in its report that these were not innocent inquiries, but were filled with "hatred and malevolence." The report ended with the hope that Viola Liuzzo had finally "found a life free of prejudice and hate."

Among the thousands of letters, though, were many profound expressions of love and sympathy, letters that consoled the family. One man, writing from Wyoming, Michigan, to the *Detroit News*, directed his letter to little Sally, who had wanted to know why her mother could

The Liuzzo home, March 30, 1965 *(The Detroit News)*

The family at the requiem mass for Viola Gregg Liuzzo (from right): husband Anthony J. Liuzzo, son Tom, son-in-law Barry Johnson, daughters Mary, Penny, and Sally and son Tony *(AP/Wide World Photos)*

not die of old age. "She died by growing up," the man wrote. "And she grew so high she reached the sky. Be proud of her," he wrote. He ended by saying, "Now your mother belongs to America. Thank you for sharing her with us."

In many letters were small contributions. A youngster sent a ten-dollar bill with a note saying he had been saving for a new pair of shoes but he thought the Liuzzo family needed the money more than he did. Mr. Liuzzo, writing to thank him, returned the money and sent the youngster a contribution for a pair of shoes.

The final rites for Mrs. Liuzzo were held at the family place of worship, the Immaculate Heart of Mary Roman Catholic Church. A capacity crowd of family, friends, neighbors, and dignitaries filled the church, while outside hundreds more crowded the sidewalk. Among the officials who came to pay their respects were Congressman Charles C. Diggs and union officers Walter Reuther and James Hoffa. Also present were James Farmer, Roy Wilkins, and Dr. King, who flew to Detroit from Atlanta to be one of the speakers.

In his eulogy the Reverend James Sheehan of the Committee on Human Rights said that the torch Mrs. Liuzzo had carried was now being picked up by people throughout the country "who felt guilt" for their racist brothers and sisters.

An unexpected speaker was Jim Letherer, who had marched with Mrs. Liuzzo to Montgomery. "I knew she didn't die in vain," he said, "because before she died, there were thousands of people sitting on the fence, trying to decide when the time was right to join the civil rights fight. Well, she proved the time is now," he said.

In Selma African-American and white mourners marched to protest the murder. A memorial meeting was also held at a small country church in Lowndes County near the site where she was killed. One hundred and fifty people crowded into the church while hundreds more stood outside. Students at Wayne State University held their own memorial meeting. And in churches all over Detroit, Viola Liuzzo was mourned and memorialized.

The nation hailed Mrs. Liuzzo as a true hero. An article in the *Michigan Chronicle* wrote of her as a woman who "reached a peak of immortality on that night."

CHAPTER ELEVEN

THE KU KLUX KLAN

Sixteen hours after the murder of Viola Gregg Liuzzo, the president of the United States informed the nation of the role of four Ku Klux Klan members in her death. Millions awakened to the dangers of the hooded group. Who were they? How did they get so powerful?

The Klan had an uneven history, flourishing during some years and fading away in others. It had its beginnings in a social club after the defeat of the Confederacy in the Civil War. Former Confederate soldiers, angry over the southern defeat, flocked to the new club, drawn to its rituals and its privacy. From its founding it was a secret society whose members wore white sheets, masks, and pointed hoods. Soon after the Civil War, the organization embarked on a program to strengthen white supremacy by overturning the gains of Reconstruction, which were giving newly freed African Americans the rights of citizenship.

Klan members wanted the United States to become a stronghold for white Christians only. To achieve their goal, they resorted to cold-blooded violence, flogging and killing people because they did not like the color of their skin or their religion. The main targets of their hatred were African Americans. They succeeded in wiping out the post-Civil War gains of newly freed slaves, barring them from voting polls and making segregation a way of life in the South.

KKK violence forced Congress to act, and in 1871 it passed an anti-Klan law. But by then southern state governments were rallying from their defeat in the Civil War. They gradually won back their authority and legal right to enforce segregation and the Klan was no longer necessary to do the job.

In the early part of the twentieth century, the Klan had a rebirth. It came in response to the mass immigration to the United States from all parts of Europe. The Klan loathed the newcomers from southern and eastern Europe: Italians, Turks, Greeks, Russian Jews, Romanians, and Hungarians. They considered them ignorant and coarse, people who would affect the American stock and make it inferior.

The early part of the century also saw a coalition of African Americans and whites push through progressive legislation. To defeat the upsurge, southern states passed stiff laws to keep blacks in their place.

In the 1920s the Klan regrouped and initiated a new campaign to combat what they called "un-American" radicalism. They saw danger in new political movements with names such as "Bolshevik," "anarchist," and "pacifist." They were now not only anti-African American but also anti-Jewish and anti-Catholic. Their ideal was a white Protestant nation. With 100,000 members, the invisible KKK empire became a government unto itself. A new wave of KKK violence spread across rural southern states, striking terror through intimidation, floggings, and lynchings. At its height in 1924, 40,000 members of the Klan, men and women, paraded down the main street of Washington, D.C.

Again public outrage brought about the decrease in Klan popularity, while internal disputes further weakened the organization.

In the 1950s and 1960s, the Klan reemerged in answer to the civil rights movement. Its tactics were unchanged, terrorizing African Americans who tried to register to vote or to win equal rights. Caught in its net were whites who came south to help in the struggle.

In February 1961 a splinter group formed the United Klans of America, Inc., Knights of the Ku Klux Klan, which eventually became the nation's largest Klan group. Like other Klan groups, its avowed purpose was the promotion of "Americanism," white supremacy, and the segregation of the races.

The four men named by the president in his television address to the nation after the Viola Liuzzo murder were members of the Alabama branch of the United Klans organization. They were Eugene Thomas, age forty-three, a steelworker, of Bessemer; William Orville Eaton, forty-one, a retired steelworker, also of Bessemer; Gary Thomas Rowe, Jr., thirty-four, unemployed, of Birmingham; and Collie Leroy Wilkins, Jr., twenty-one, an automobile mechanic, of Fairfield.

The speedy arrest of the four men was explained by a startling revelation. It was disclosed that one of the four, Gary Thomas Rowe, Jr., was not only a member of the Klan but also an undercover informant for the FBI, a dual role he played for five years. Rowe had joined the Klan when he moved to Birmingham from Atlanta, Georgia, where he was born. In Birmingham he was recruited as an informant. On the evening of the murder, Rowe called the Birmingham office of the FBI to inform them that he was one of the four men in the car that had gunned down a woman. When his role as a paid informant became public, Rowe was placed in protective custody and his family spirited away into seclusion.

Therefore, only three men were indicted by the state of Alabama on first-degree murder charges in the Liuzzo slaying. All were released on $50,000 bond each. They were also indicted on a federal charge of conspiring to violate Mrs. Liuzzo's civil rights and released on $10,000 bond each for that charge. Thus the men were under two indictments: a state charge of murder and a federal charge of violation of civil rights.

The arrests of the Klansmen set in motion a new set of media stories. A banner headline in the *Detroit News* announced, WILL ASK CHAIR IN SLAYING, ALABAMA SAYS. According to the news story, the Alabama attorney general, Richmond Flowers, was expected to ask for the death penalty for the Klansmen for the slaying of civil rights worker Viola Liuzzo. "There will be no sweeping under the rug or whitewashing of this case," Flowers promised.

While the attorney general was making his accusations, the Klan lawyer, Matt H. Murphy, Jr., accused the national government of bribing Gary Thomas Rowe, Jr., in order to get him to inform. Also speaking out in defense of the Klan was Robert Shelton, Jr., of Tuscaloosa, Imperial Wizard of the United Klans of America, Inc. At a news conference, he admitted that the Klan had posted bond for the three indicted men. He also vented his rage at President Johnson, calling him "a liar" for referring to the Klan as a bunch of "hooded bigots."

The trial of the three Klansmen got under way on May 3 in Hayneville, seat of Lowndes County. Television crews, reporters, and photographers from across the United States and around the world turned the rural town into a bustling center of activity. New telephone wires were strung and sound trucks filled the town square for the immediate relay of news.

On the second floor of the hundred-year-old white stone courthouse, a jury was being selected to hear the trial of Collie Leroy Wilkins, Jr., the youngest of the three Klan members, for the murder of Viola Liuzzo.

A careful check had been made by the FBI of the hundred members on the jury panel to eliminate anyone connected to the Klan. After twelve white men were finally selected, the Wilkins trial started. His defense attorney was six-foot-three Matt Murphy, Jr., the Imperial Klonsel of the Knights of the Ku Klux Klan.

Testimony started on Tuesday, May 4. First on the witness stand were state troopers, who described finding the body. The medical examiner then reported that death was caused by bullets piercing the victim's skull.

A key prosecution witness was Leroy Moton, the young man who had been riding alongside Mrs. Liuzzo when she was murdered. In a barely audible voice, the frightened Mr. Moton explained that he and Mrs. Liuzzo had ferried a group of marchers from Montgomery back to Selma on March 25 and that they were en route back to Montgomery a bit after 7:30 P.M. that same evening to pick up another group of marchers. Mrs. Liuzzo, he recalled, was humming "We Shall Overcome" when another car pulled up alongside theirs on Route 80. Shots rang out, two or three, Moton said. The car plunged off the road. Mr. Moton described how he had turned off the lights of the car and waited five minutes. Soon the car that had fired the shots came back, shone lights into the Liuzzo car, and drove off. Moton then tried to hail a passing car, he said, but after a few minutes, feeling faint from the accident, he returned to the car and passed out for twenty-five to thirty minutes. Then again he was on the road, running, and this time he succeeded in stopping a truck that belonged to the civil rights movement, which drove him back to town.

The Klan's strategy was clear from the beginning: to turn the truth upside down. Murphy tried to get Moton to admit that he was the one who had the gun, that he tried to rob Mrs. Liuzzo and shot through the window to make it look like an outside job. When Moton remained firm in his testimony, Murphy tried to get him to say that he and Mrs. Liuzzo had a sexual relationship, that Mrs. Liuzzo was a communist, a radical, and morally irresponsible. Moton again firmly denied the accusations.

The witness who drew the greatest attention was Gary Thomas Rowe, Jr. For being a government witness, he was granted immunity from prosecution. The redheaded Mr. Rowe was a figure in a "cloak-and-dagger" scenario, surrounded by tight security as he entered the back door of the courthouse. He told a gripping story revealing insights into the working of the Klan. He testified that he had received a phone call from his superior in the Klan on the evening of March 24 instructing him to make the trip to Montgomery the next day. The four men were therefore on assignment when they met and drove the hundred miles from Birmingham to Montgomery, where they spent the day. At 6:20 P.M., on the way to Selma, they got a ticket for driving their car with a noisy muffler. At 6:35 P.M. the men stopped at the Silver Moon Café in Selma, where Thomas and Rowe had two beers each. They had had other beers during the day.

Thomas was driving the car; Eaton sat next to him. In the back seat were Rowe on the left and Wilkins on the right. The four drove to Selma from Montgomery and were headed out of town when they stopped at a traffic light. It was then that they noticed the blue Oldsmobile sedan with a white woman driver and an African-American man seated next to her.

Wilkins pointed to the Oldsmobile and said, "Looka there, Baby Brother. I'll be damned, looka there." They all looked.

"Let's get them," said Eugene Thomas. At that point they began to follow the Liuzzo car onto U.S. Route 80. Three times they tried to overtake the car but had to draw back. The first time they saw a jeepful of army military police; the second time they saw two highway patrol cars; the third time a couple of trucks got in the way.

By that time Mrs. Liuzzo was aware she was being

followed and increased her speed to eighty, ninety miles an hour. But the Klan car kept up with her, following her onto the two-lane highway of Lowndes County. Near a swampy area, the Klan car drove up alongside the Liuzzo car. Rowe vividly described what then took place. He saw Wilkins thrust a .38 caliber pistol out of the right rear window. He described how the Klan car pulled ahead so that the back window of its car was alongside the front window of the Liuzzo car, how Mrs. Liuzzo at that moment turned around and looked directly at them, and how at that instant Wilkins fired two shots through the window of the blue Oldsmobile. The driver of the Klan car, Eugene Thomas, shouted, "All right, men, shoot the hell out of them," and everyone shot at the car, emptying their guns. A total of twelve shots was fired.

Rowe insisted he only pretended to shoot. After the shooting, he said, the Klan car returned to Montgomery and then went on to Birmingham. There Rowe left the others, found a telephone, and called the FBI to report the murder.

Defense counsel Murphy wasted no time in trying to break down Rowe's testimony, calling him a "paid informant and a pimp." At one point Murphy asked Rowe whether he was a paid agent of Fidel Castro (president of Cuba) or whether he was a member of the NAACP. Finally Murphy shot the crucial question to Rowe, "You didn't do anything to prevent the firing of the shots?"

"No, sir," said Rowe. "I didn't know the shots were going to be fired until they were fired," was Rowe's answer.

Defendant Wilkins never took the stand. His plea from the beginning was Not Guilty. He sat in front of the courtroom, appearing sleepy and at other times bored or indifferent, as his case for murder was being tried.

The case was turned over to the jury on May 5 after summations by Matt Murphy, Jr., for the defense, and attorneys for the prosecution. Murphy often wore on his left lapel a small red Ku Klux Klan insignia and a NEVER button. The button was an answer to the question "Desegregate?" In the courtroom was Imperial Wizard Robert Shelton, as well as Robert Creel, Klan Grand Dragon of the Atlanta Realm. Sheriff Jim Clark was there at the beginning of the trial. Throughout the hearings other Klan members filled the courtroom.

Murphy's hour-long closing arguments were in turn angry, defiant, and blustering. He argued that the civil rights movement was communistic and offered a generalized attack on all Negroes, Zionists, and civil rights workers. At one time he thundered, "I am proud to stand on my feet and say that I am for white supremacy."

In his key argument, Murphy attacked the credibility of the FBI witness, Gary Thomas Rowe, Jr., calling him a "liar and a perjurer." His greatest scorn was reserved for what Murphy called Rowe's betrayal of the Klan, and for being "a part of a grand conspiracy to destroy the United Klans of America and the South." In a heated moment, he accused Rowe of being an accomplice to the murder.

Arguing the case for the government was Circuit Solicitor Arthur E. Gamble, along with the assistant state attorney general, Joseph B. Gantt, and the solicitor, Carlton L. Perdue. They argued that even Governor Wallace had said that the Liuzzo murder was "a cowardly act that should not go unpunished." They spoke against anarchy and against lawlessness. Referring to the murder of a defenseless woman, Gantt asked, "Is this what our forefathers fought for in the Civil War—this kind of bravery; the kind that it takes to shoot down a defenseless woman?" No one has the right to kill, said Gantt, because that person is enraged at the sight of a white woman and a Negro man sitting alongside each other in an automobile.

In the heat of the final arguments, Mrs. Liuzzo was almost forgotten. It had become a case of white supremacy against the rights of African Americans. Even the chief prosecutor, Arthur Gamble, did nothing to create sympathy for the murdered woman. Her effects were carelessly lying around the courtroom, stacked in four cardboard boxes, a satchel, and a briefcase. A sociology textbook was on top of one of the cartons, and her tan pocketbook was on the floor. Inside the pocketbook was a card donating her eyes to the Wayne State University Eye Bank.

After deliberating for ten hours over two days, the jury reported back to the court and declared itself hopelessly deadlocked. Circuit Judge Werth Thagard declared a mistrial and dismissed the Lowndes County jury on May 7.

In polling the jurors, the judge learned that ten were for conviction and two for acquittal. A unanimous verdict was required for either conviction or acquittal.

A new trial was planned for the fall.

CHAPTER TWELVE

THE VERDICT

In response to the Viola Liuzzo murder, SNCC took its voter registration drive to Lowndes County, where not a single African American had registered to vote since Reconstruction. Under the leadership of Stokely Carmichael, activists moved into the terrorized, Klan-controlled county to get black citizens ready for the difficult registration process. On May 3, the day the Liuzzo trial opened in Hayneville, 150 African Americans appeared at the registration office, only to be frustrated by the complex questionnaire and the usual obstacles put in their way. After two months of hard work, only five people were added to the voting rolls. The taxing, unsuccessful process forced civil rights workers to put more pressure on the federal government. Only a voting rights bill, they said, would give *all* people equal access to the ballot.

In answer to the expanded voter registration drive,

Klan activity increased. The local heroes at Klan events were the three men indicted for the Liuzzo murder. They traveled through the South to win new members for the Klan. Wilkins and William Eaton were honored at a Klan parade of 500 through the streets of Atlanta, Georgia. At the rally in the local park, the keynote speaker was Imperial Klan Klonsel Matt Murphy.

Klan terror in the South could not drown out the voices of tens of thousands demanding that Congress pass a voting rights bill. The small town of Selma had charged the country with its passion. The highly dramatic protests had peaked in Bloody Sunday, the march to Montgomery, and the murder of three civil rights workers: Jimmie Lee Jackson, the Reverend James Reeb, and Viola Liuzzo. The relentless pressure of African Americans mandated change.

The upsurge finally resulted in federal action. On Friday, August 6, President Johnson, in a televised ceremony, signed the Voting Rights Act into law.

Under the new act, the unfair literacy tests were outlawed. To guarantee equal access to the ballot, federal registrars would oversee the elections in six southern states. The Voting Rights Act gave the civil rights movement one of its most dramatic victories.

The federal government also moved on another front, holding public hearings to make visible "the invisible empire of the Ku Klux Klan." The investigation followed President Johnson's demand after the Liuzzo murder that legislation be drafted to permit the federal government to move against the secret organization.

In October 1965 the second Wilkins trial opened in Hayneville. Each side was represented by a new set of attorneys. Attorney General Richmond M. Flowers, known as a racial moderate, replaced Arthur E. Gamble. Arthur Hanes, a former mayor of Birmingham, replaced Matt Murphy, who was killed in an automobile accident in August.

In a report issued on the evening of the trial, Flowers placed the responsibility for the Klan violence on Governor Wallace for doing nothing to curb the organization. Flowers received death threats during this period, as did others who stood up to the Klan.

In trying to expose the racism of the jury system, Flowers exposed the system itself, showing how a jury was kept all white even where blacks outnumbered whites four to one. In the questioning of prospective jurors, a few whites admitted that "they believed white civil rights workers to be inferior to other white persons." Others admitted they believed in white supremacy. It seemed impossible to get an unbiased jury.

Nevertheless a jury was finally selected and the second trial of Collie Leroy Wilkins, Jr., for the murder of Viola Liuzzo opened. Again the star witness was FBI informer Gary Thomas Rowe, Jr. Again he described being sent on the mission by a Klan superior who phoned him early on March 25 and told him to go to Montgomery, where the Selma to Montgomery march would end. He repeated the testimony he gave at the first Wilkins trial about how Wilkins shot Mrs. Liuzzo.

In his summation Attorney General Flowers pleaded for a guilty verdict, saying, "The blood of this man's [Wilkins's] sin, if you do not find him guilty, will stain every soul of our country for an eternity."

Defense attorney Arthur Hanes, in his summation,

attacked Rowe's credibility, saying, "He sells information for money. If there is no information, he makes, he fabricates information and then he goes and peddles it."

The case went to the jury on October 22. After one hour and thirty-five minutes of deliberation, the jury filed back into the courtroom and announced its decision. Not guilty. Several white spectators in the courtroom burst into applause.

But the legal trials of the three Klansmen were not over. They still faced federal charges of conspiracy to violate the civil rights of Viola Liuzzo.

The federal case was tried before Judge Frank M. Johnson in the United States District Court in Montgomery. After the selection of an all-white jury, Judge Johnson cautioned jury members to "rid their minds of preconceived ideas and strive for a fair verdict."

Leading the federal prosecution was John M. Doar, head of the Justice Department's civil rights division. He came from Washington to handle the case. In his arguments Doar tried to show that the United Klans of America, Inc., Knights of the Ku Klux Klan, was involved in a conspiracy to deprive Mrs. Liuzzo and others of their civil rights. Such an act, said Mr. Doar, was a felony, or serious crime, according to an 1870 law passed during Reconstruction. Mrs. Liuzzo and other marchers, said Mr. Doar, were protected because the march had been approved by a federal court.

In this case informant Gary Thomas Rowe, Jr., described in fuller detail how his instructions to go to Montgomery had come from Robert Thomas, Grand Titan of the Klan for the Birmingham area. He explained further how those instructions in turn had been handed down to Thomas by the Imperial Wizard, Robert Shelton.

Rowe's testimony made it clear that the four men had been instructed to go to Montgomery and find someone to punish, anyone who had taken part in the Selma to Montgomery march. Mrs. Liuzzo had been selected at random.

Once again Rowe repeated his story of the killing. Under Doar's careful questioning, Rowe said the purpose of the Klan was "to maintain white supremacy," and to do so by "any means necessary, whether bullets or ballots."

Defense lawyer Hanes did not succeed in shaking Rowe's testimony. Jury members deliberated for a day and a half and at one point reported that they were hopelessly deadlocked. Judge Johnson sent them back to the jury room, sternly ordering them to try again. On the afternoon of Friday, December 3, the jury returned to court with a verdict. It found the defendants guilty of conspiracy to violate the civil rights of Mrs. Viola Gregg Liuzzo, leading to her murder.

Judge Johnson sentenced the Klansmen to the maximum sentence, ten years in prison. Afterward the judge commented to the jurors that, in his opinion, the guilty verdict was the only fair decision possible. The sentence was upheld after an appeal.

The conviction of the Klansmen, so rare in southern courts, startled many people, especially civil rights workers. They had not expected a fair verdict. The conviction and sentences were landmarks in southern racial history.

The three Klansmen facing trial on federal charges of conspiracy in the Federal Courthouse lobby (from left): Eugene Thomas, Collie Leroy Wilkins, Jr., and William O. Eaton. The others are unidentified. *(The Montgomery Advertiser)*

CHAPTER THIRTEEN

THE AFTERMATH

Mr. Liuzzo and the children welcomed the final verdict. They had been bewildered and angered when the two trials of Collie Leroy Wilkins, Jr., had at first resulted in a hung jury, and then in a verdict of not guilty. Though disappointed that the three Klansmen, Wilkins, Eugene Thomas, and William Orville, were not convicted of murder, at least the family knew that the murderers were behind bars.

Family members had had little peace. They not only had to deal with the sudden death of a young wife and mother, but they had to deal with *murder*. The trials, which went on for seven months, kept them in the public eye. Complicating their lives throughout was the bigotry, the racial prejudice, that hounded them.

Only one day after the funeral service, a burned cross was found in the family's backyard. To protect his children, Mr. Liuzzo arranged for a security guard to watch the house. The Detroit police also kept an eye on the Liuzzo home. At night phone calls awakened the family to drunken voices on the line shouting obscenities and threats.

Then there was the prying into their personal lives. Reporters dug into old newspaper files and court records. They wrote about the year Mrs. Liuzzo had kept the children out of school and the subsequent court case and police record. They found out about the time she had vanished for a few days and the police were alerted. Even private family matters, unrelated to the case, were written about for the gossip mill.

While the outside world was making its peace with the Liuzzo murder in its own way, the personal world of the Liuzzo family trembled with shock and uncertainty. Nothing would ever be the same. Viola Liuzzo, so eager, so full of energy, and so full of love, had filled the household with a bright light. Exuberant about her own future, she inspired her children to dream of theirs, to make their lives exciting and adventurous. But now the poetry and dreams were stilled, and the memories of their mother were also stilled, capturing her forever young, brave, kind, and strong. They remembered how she brought home those who needed help, and how she spoke tirelessly about people, teaching them that "everybody is equal and entitled to equal treatment, whether they are black, white, Jew, or Gentile."

Though other family members tried to protect the children, they nevertheless found themselves in situations difficult to understand, such as having to account to reporters and strangers for their feelings and thoughts. There was no one to tell them how to deal

105

with the media, or with gossip, or with racial hatred—a hatred so violent that it could kill.

Jim Liuzzo's grief and rage never subsided and he stormed at the evil men who had ambushed and murdered his wife. He would remember her phone call the last evening. "I'm very happy. Don't worry. I love you." He would recall that his wife was one "who fought for everyone's rights; she was the champion of the underdog." And because she thought people's rights were being violated in Selma, she had to do something about it.

He and the family pulled together to start the healing process. Instead of attending important business meetings each evening, Mr. Liuzzo came home, and he also spent weekends with the children. Sarah Evans became a mainstay, a figure of towering love. Oldest daughter Penny, remembering how much her mother valued education, planned to enter a community college. Mary's marriage broke up and she returned to Detroit to live with the family. Teenage Tommy, who had been closest to his mother, withdrew into his own world. Young Tony, called Nino, was inconsolable, weeping in his pain. Six-year-old Sally still expected her mother to walk in the front door.

The time came when the family tried to resume normal lives. For the young children it meant a return to school in the fall of 1965. Sally never forgot that September day when she walked to school. She was then seven years old. Neighbors stood outside their homes, calling her names as she passed by. "Nigger lover's baby," was the one she remembered most clearly, as she recalled the twisted expressions of hatred on their faces.

Tony, in his first days back at school, was beaten up and also called a "nigger lover."

Later that fall Mr. Liuzzo removed his children from the neighborhood public school and placed them in a Catholic school, where he hoped they would be spared additional violence and abuse.

But no matter where the children attended school or lived, their names were public. Tony would say in later years, "I've been labeled all my life a 'nigger lover' because of what my mother did. If that's what I am, then God love it."

Sally, too, would recall that life was never able to resume a normal course. Each time Wilkins and the other Klansmen were on trial, the family was besieged by reporters and photographers. They had to listen to the nasty accusations against their mother by the Klan lawyer. They had to listen to her character slandered, hearing that she was a morally loose woman, that she was irresponsible for leaving five children and going down south to join a risky struggle.

Why so much criticism? They could not understand it. Because she was a woman? A white woman who helped in the black civil rights movement? In Sally's view her mother was heroic and courageous, and the family was proud of her.

After a year or so, public criticism died down. Penny could report that schoolmates would come up to her and say, "I'm awfully sorry about your mother." Her biology teacher took her aside and told her, "Well, you have a lot of friends in the world." And those friends continued to grow in number.

The children could deal with the knowledge that their

lives were thrown off course, and that Tommy and Tony dropped out of school, a thing their mother would not have permitted, said Tony. They were learning to live with the unending pain of missing their mother. The memory of her—a hero in the best tradition—fortified them. They defended her right to her point of view and her right to become active on behalf of equality and justice for all people. They just wished she had not died in vain, that the country had learned from the struggles in the South and that racism was a thing of the past, that hate groups could no longer practice their deadly terror and violence. The drama and passions of the African-American struggles in Selma to which their mother gave her life and for which she is valued are more meaningful to them than nasty racist voices.

They appreciate the fact that their mother's murder hastened the passage of the Voting Rights Act in August 1965. Within a few months, a tide of African Americans and other minorities flooded local courthouses to register to vote. Within ten years after the law was enacted, African-American registration in Selma jumped from 2 percent to 60 percent. In the South as a whole, registration increased to over 60 percent from less than 40 percent. The empowerment of African-American voters brought about basic changes in economic and political life. A *New York Times* article in May 1992 reported, AFTER 115 YEARS, A BLACK WILL REPRESENT ALABAMA in the U.S. Congress. "There has been a growing tide of black political activity in Alabama since the Voting Rights Act of 1965," the report went on to say. "That activity has produced 705 current black elected officials in the state, giving Alabama the largest number of black legislators, school board members, mayors, council members, sheriffs, and county commissioners of any state."

Viola Liuzzo contributed to the empowerment of African Americans. Her martyrdom is enshrined forever in the Civil Rights Memorial in Montgomery. At the plaza in front of the Southern Poverty Law Center, her name is engraved in black granite as one of those who gave their lives for the cause of African-American liberation.

At the site where she was killed on U.S. Route 80, the women of the Southern Christian Leadership Conference dedicated a stone marker in 1989: IN MEMORY OF OUR SISTER VIOLA LIUZZO. Each year the Civil Rights Educational Heritage Tour, led by Mrs. Evelyn Lowery of the SCLC, stops at the site of the murder to hold a memorial service. The two or three busloads of students and other visitors who make up the tour learn about the historic march and the murder of Viola Liuzzo.

In May 1982 the Detroit City Council passed a Testimonial Resolution to the memory of Mrs. Viola Liuzzo "because we, like all right-thinking citizens, will never forget the magnificent contributions she made to the struggle for civil and human rights."

In June of that year, the Office of the Mayor of the City of Detroit issued a proclamation making June 1–8, 1982, Viola Liuzzo Commemoration Week. The proclamation also honored Mrs. Liuzzo's son Tony for "carrying on with his mother's commitment to equality." Tony, who took up his mother's torch, helped organize a motorcade to Washington, D.C., in 1982 to demonstrate for the renewal of the federal Voting Rights Act, which was due to expire that year.

Mrs. Evelyn Lowery of the SCLC and Lowndes County Sheriff John Hulett at a prayer service for Viola Liuzzo at the site of her murder *(The Montgomery Advertiser)*

It was Tony who went down to Selma in February 1982 to march with one hundred others to Montgomery in a reenactment of the 1965 march. Thousands joined the marchers for a day, but Tony was among the one hundred who logged the full fifty-four miles on foot. After two days of walking along Route 80, they came to the spot in Lowndes County where Tony's mother was killed. Tears rolled down his face as he climbed across the ditch and up the embankment where marchers had placed a wreath. Tony sobbed; so did many others.

In his remarks Tony said how difficult the moment was for him. "But the spirit of my mother, of Martin Luther King, and every brave soul who lay down their lives for freedom are with us today. We will pick up the trail and march on."

Tony Liuzzo placing a wreath at the site of his mother's murder during the reenactment of the march to Montgomery in 1982 *(The Montgomery Advertiser)*

A statue of Martin Luther King, Jr., in front of Brown Chapel memorializes the three who gave their lives in the struggle for voting rights. *(Courtesy Selma–Dallas County Chamber of Commerce)*

EPILOGUE

Questions that were essentially unanswered continued to bewilder the Liuzzo family. Why didn't Rowe, an FBI informant, prevent the murder? Didn't he have a moral obligation to do so?

The family thought they found some answers when in December 1975, a U.S. Senate subcommittee held hearings that revealed new information. The hearings dealt with the roles of the FBI and the CIA (Central Intelligence Agency) and the possible abuses of power by their agents investigating political activists in the 1960s. In the course of the hearings, it was revealed that Gary Thomas Rowe, Jr., may have participated in several acts of violence while he was an FBI informant. In one confrontation he was suspected of involvement in the savage beating of Freedom Riders in Anniston, Alabama, in 1961. He also may have been involved in the church bombing that killed four African-American children in Birmingham, Alabama, in 1963. He had, it was claimed, notified the FBI of many violent acts planned by the Klan, but the agency did not always act on his information. Only in two instances did it intervene to prevent violence.

On the day Viola Liuzzo was murdered, Rowe notified the FBI that he was going out with other Klansmen and that an act of violence was planned.

These revelations shocked the nation but none were more shocked than the children of Viola Liuzzo. Did their mother have to die? Why did the FBI not try to prevent the violence? And was it possible that Rowe himself may have pulled the trigger?

The family requested and finally received the government documents related to the case. The disclosures forced the family to act. In 1979 they filed a $2 million lawsuit against the federal government. The lawsuit claimed that the FBI did nothing to prevent the mission of violence on which Rowe was sent by the

Klan. The Detroit American Civil Liberties Union attorney Jack Novik, representing the Liuzzo family, considered Rowe an "active participant" in the murder, if not "the actual murderer."

An Alabama grand jury indicted Rowe for the Liuzzo murder and he was arrested in his Georgia hideout.

Tony Liuzzo said the family originally accepted the official version of the slaying but in 1975, the U.S. Senate subcommittee hearings changed their perspective. The evidence of Rowe's participation in Klan violence convinced them that the government was responsible, that there had been government negligence.

Jim Liuzzo was spared much of the heartache to come. In 1978 he died from the effects of a stroke.

Tony Liuzzo, now the family spokesperson, and other family members worked hard on the case. They were sure their lawyers could prove the government was, at the very least, responsible for negligence.

The case was heard in March 1983 before Federal District Judge Charles Joiner. It was not a jury trial so the verdict was completely in the hands of the judge. He handed down his decision in the spring of 1983. He found that Rowe did not shoot Mrs. Liuzzo and that the government was not responsible for the murder of Mrs. Liuzzo.

The Liuzzo children were unprepared for the decision. They had fully expected that justice would be on their side. Even their lawyers were amazed at the verdict. Not only did the family lose the case, but the court, in an unusual move, fined the family $79,800 for court costs.

Tony Liuzzo said, "They'll have to drag me to jail before I'd pay a penny. . . . I will never pay a penny to the United States government for the murder of my mother, and for bringing action to find out exactly what happened to my mother."

The American Civil Liberties Union appealed the verdict of court costs on behalf of the family and succeeded in getting the fine for expenses voided.

A NATIONAL HISTORIC TRAIL

Under study is a proposal to make the route of the Selma to Montgomery march in 1965 a national historic trail. The U.S. Congress in 1990 directed the National Park Service to study the route to see whether it is of sufficient national significance in American history to merit historic preservation. The proposed trail would incorporate the site of the murder of Viola Gregg Liuzzo, weaving her life into African-American history and the dramatic struggle for civil rights.

The Planning and Federal Programs Division of the National Park Service in Atlanta, Georgia, distributes material about the project. Their booklet, *Selma to Montgomery*, includes a map, a brief history of the march, a discussion of alternate plans to celebrate it, and a call for public reactions to the proposal.

ACKNOWLEDGMENTS

Members of the Liuzzo family and many others shared with me their knowledge and insights during my visits to Detroit, Michigan, and to Selma and Montgomery, Alabama. In personal and telephone interviews, the Liuzzo children once again recalled the painful events of previous decades. I would like to express my special gratitude to Sally Prado, Penellipi Herrington, Mary Eva Ashley, and for a few brief phone talks, to Anthony Liuzzo, Jr. Above all, my thanks to Mrs. Sarah Evans for her unfailing kindness and patience.

I would also like to thank the following members of the clergy for sharing with me their special understanding: the Reverends Jack Mendelsohn, Nancy Doughty, Rudolph Gelsey, Malcolm Boyd, and Father Tim Deasy.

J. T. Johnson of the Southern Christian Leadership Conference staff, Mrs. Amelia Boynton Robinson, Mrs. Alice West, Allston Fitts III of the Edmundite Missions, and many others added their experience and knowledge of the events in Selma and the great march: To all of them I am most grateful.

Too numerous to specify but whose experiences were helpful, I would like to thank former faculty and students at Wayne State University who recalled the dramatic campus and city protests of 1965. I am indebted to David Garrow for reading the manuscript and giving me the benefit of his scholarship.

Finally I would like to thank Dr. June Finer, a member of the medical personnel, and Trudy Orris for telling me how it was to be part of the Selma to Montgomery march.

BIBLIOGRAPHY

A vast literature has grown up around the civil rights movement in general and about the Selma to Montgomery march in particular. These books, however, deal with the murder of Viola Liuzzo in a sentence or two, sometimes in a paragraph. A chapter is devoted to her life and death only in Jack Mendelsohn's book *The Martyrs: 16 Who Gave Their Lives for Racial Justice* (New York: Harper & Row, 1966). My research therefore centered on the extensive newspaper and magazine coverage of the time and on personal interviews. Providing information was Anthony Ripley's "The Enigma of Mrs. Liuzzo," in the *Detroit News* (May 23, 1965). Ken Fireman's lengthy article in the *Detroit Free Press* (April 25, 1982) titled "Babe, I'm Going to Alabama," is an insightful study of Anthony Liuzzo, Jr.

Giving an in-depth study of the march are Charles E. Fager's *Selma, 1965: The March That Changed the South* (Boston: Beacon Press, 1974, 1985) and David Garrow's *Protest at Selma: Martin Luther King, Jr., and the Voting Rights Act of 1965* (New Haven: Yale University Press, 1978).

Contributing to my understanding of the period was James Forman's *Sammy Younge, Jr.: The First Black College Student to Die in the Black Liberation Movement* (New York: Grove Press, 1968).

Of great interest was "The FBI File on the KKK Murder of Viola Liuzzo," a microform publication by Scholarly Resources, Inc. (made available through interlibrary loan by the New York Public Library). Though heavily censored, the file reveals the detailed FBI investigation into the murder and its particular perspective on events.

An unexpected resource has been the Museum of Television and Radio in New York City, where I was able to listen to

President Johnson deliver his speech to Congress on the voting rights bill on March 15, 1965, and where I also viewed the great march as it left St. Jude's and entered the large plaza in front of the state capitol in Montgomery.

Invaluable were the newspaper and magazine articles of the period. The on-the-spot reporting communicated the immediacy of events in the liberation struggle. The articles are too numerous to list, but *Ebony* magazine's Simeon Booker, in his story "50,000 March on Montgomery" (May 1965), catches the fire and spirit of the great walk. So does Renata Adler in "Letter from Selma" (*New Yorker,* April 10, 1965). Jimmy Breslin's report can be found in *The World of Jimmy Breslin* (New York: Viking Press, 1967). Periodicals such as *Life, Newsweek,* and *Jet,* among others, provide excellent photographs and news coverage of the dramatic events as they unfolded.

SUGGESTED TITLES FOR YOUNG READERS

Alvarez, Joseph A. *From Reconstruction to Revolution: The Blacks' Struggle for Equality.* New York: Atheneum, 1971.

Cook, Fred J. *The Ku Klux Klan: America's Recurring Nightmare.* New York: Julian Messner, 1980.

Miller, Marilyn. *The Bridge at Selma.* Morristown, N.J.: Silver Burdett Press, 1985.

Severn, Bill. *The Right to Vote.* New York: Ives Washburn, 1972.

Siegel, Beatrice. *The Year They Walked: Rosa Parks and the Montgomery Bus Boycott.* New York: Four Winds Press, 1992.

Webb, Sheyann, and Rachel West Nelson. *Selma, Lord, Selma: Girlhood Memories of the Civil Rights Days* as told to Frank Sikora. Tuscaloosa, Ala.: University of Alabama Press, 1980.

INDEX

921
.LIU

Siegel, Beatrice

Murder on the
 highway

$14.95

33044000575596